Discoveri ~ Its History, Myths & Curiosities

by

Robert Jeffery

Published by Robert Jeffery for the Tong Parochial Church Council
Tong Vicarage, Tong, Shifnal, Shropshire TF11 8PW.

ISBN 987-0-9555089-0-5

Printed by Parchment (Oxford) Ltd.,
1a, Crescent Road, Cowley, Oxford. OX4 9PB

**All profits from the sale of this book will be contributed to the
maintenance of the fabric of St Bartholomew's Church, Tong.**

Contents

4

Acknowledgements

This book has been over 20 years in the making. I hope that this final result is a worthy successor to Griffiths' *History of Tong and Boscobel* published 110 years ago. That was a strange and rather bitty book, with a lot of data, not very well organised. Yet it is one of the three main sources for this book. The second was the J. E. Auden's *Notes on the History of Tong*. I am grateful to George and Joyce Frost, who subsequently transcribed them and had them published. Auden was a careful and reliable historian. The third was the Durant Family Papers.

Since I stared on this material much more has emerged and I am deeply grateful to Robert Stallard, son of a former Churchwarden of Tong who has dedicated a lot of time to digging away at the census figures, the National Archives at Kew and in many other places. He and I have shared many ideas and speculations in the process, but the book would not be what it is without his work and his highly skilled technical knowledge of computers. Robert first got involved though sharing in the archaeological excavations at Tong conducted by Alan Wharton whose campaigning and pioneering work revealed much about Tong that had never been known before and he was generous with his time and energy. The late Philip Barker, Consultant archaeologist to Worcester Cathedral and a former lecturer at Birmingham University, who worked for years on the Roman site at Wroxeter, read the first draft and made many helpful suggestions. The Notes and Bibliography reveal many of the sources for this final version, but I would like to thank the following people who have offered unstinting help and encouragement: Mr James Barth; Mr George Baugh; The Revd Charles Bradshaw; Mrs Margaret Brown; Mrs Christine Buckley; Prof Anthony Cox; Sally Ford; The Ven & Mrs George Frost; Canon and Mrs Graham Fuller; Dr Giles Gasper; The Rt Revd John Garton; The Ven John Hall; Dr Christopher Haigh; Mr & Mrs Chris Hayes; Mrs and Mrs A Hibbert-Hingston; Lady Elizabeth Higgs; the late Anna Hulbert; the late Canon Iain Mackenzie; Professor Henry Mayr-Harting; Mr Wim Meulenkamp; Mr Edward Pearce; Canon John Rogan; Revd John Salter; Canon Dr Jane Shaw; Mr Paul Stamper; Revd Preb Pippa Thorneycroft; Mr Michael Thomas; Mr A Webster (Archivist of Belvoir Castle): Mr John Whale; Mr Alan Wharton; Revd John Whitehead. Thanks also to the officers at Nottingham University Library; Lichfield Diocesan Archives; Shropshire County Archives and the National

Archive at Kew. I am grateful to my daughter, Philippa, for her drawings and to Alan Webster for his overgenerous Foreword.

Above all I would like to thank the villagers of Tong, past and present, who have sustained and continued the story of Tong. I owe a deep debt of gratitude to Anne Tuck and her late husband, Bill Tuck, who loved and cared for Tong over many years, and in whose memory this book is dedicated.

Robert Jeffery   *Oxford, January 2007*

Foreword

It has been a delight to follow the story of the midland village of Tong from Roman times, when it was a settlement on the way to the fine city of Viroconium, to the village almost crushed by the day and night traffic of the M54. The author lived here for only nine years but he clearly became devoted to the place, as have been other visitors.

An American, coming briefly from Birmingham in 1868, described the Church as a miniature cathedral as was fascinated by the school "full of ruddy rural boys and girls as happy as birds". John Betjeman wrote of the now demolished castle as "strange but romantic". Its families, especially the Vernons, Stanleys and Durants were all unusual, even eccentric; some of the Durants might have qualified as Chaplains to the Hell Fire Club or the most notorious Pirates of the Caribbean.

The Great Bell of Tong (1518) rang down the centuries. One son hated his father so thoroughly that he erected a gibbet with an effigy of his father hanging on it as a testimony of his feelings. We read of an incumbent who had bowled out W. G. Grace for 0 and Grace's brother for 2 in the same over.

I was brought up in the neighbouring County of Cheshire. I know the power and surprise of village stories. Our pub was called "Salamanca" to remind us of the Peninsular War. We all knew the true story of the British Legion official who left his signal box on the Crewe-Shrewsbury line to run across fields to catch an escaping prisoner. We admired the Vicar and a leading Methodist layman who collected enough from everyone in the community in those pre-Welfare State days, to retrain, re-house and employ a young married man, blinded at work. The parson nearby ministered faithfully, though gassed on the Somme. When we visited Chester Cathedral we were reminded of the teenager Jack Cornwell, wounded at Jutland who stayed at his post on HMS Chester maintaining communications. Midland villages deserve historians who will tell their stories, as we are here told the tales of Tong.

My favourite pastors include George Herbert, Alan Ecclestone, John Breay and Bernard Gilpin. I now add Robert Jeffery, a faithful priest and a truthful historian.

Bob Jeffery has worked in London, the provinces and the countryside. He has brought up a family, known illness and bereavement and acted as

8

curate, vicar, Archdeacon and Dean. He has cared deeply that the Church should be ecumenical, and welcomed reform, including the ministry of women and the rethinking of doctrine. He has many close friends in England and abroad and continues to travel widely overseas; he is a generous host and a skilled cook. His combination of humour, kindness and shrewd honesty is a rare achievement. When many in the mainstream churches have shrunk from taking risks, he has faced challenging decisions. His reflections on Tong, a single community surviving civil war and major religious and cultural changes, are a spur in our days of terrorism to reflect on our society's future and our need for radical realignment and local resilience.

Alan Webster KCVO
(Dean Emeritus of St Paul's)

Prologue

When I told the Bishop of Oxford (Rt. Revd Kenneth Woolcombe) that I was going to be priest-in-charge of Tong, his response was "It sounds as if you are going to be the head of a Chinese Secret society". From the first time I came on a visit, I was attracted to the village. Here I was a Londoner, who had never lived in a rural setting feeling really at home in this small village.

There are two main factors that have led to my writing this book. A friend of mine in Oxford told me that when I went to Tong, I would be surrounded by her ancestors. Later, she showed me the remarkable archive of the Durant Family Papers. This was a story that needed telling, but as I reflected on the material, it became clear that the village and the Durants were so intertwined that you could not tell the story of the one without the other. Some material was at hand in Griffiths' **History of Tong and Boscobel**, and in a pile of papers and old notebooks that I found in the Parish Chest. Then I came across the Revd J. E. Auden's handwritten **Notes on the History of Tong** in the Shropshire Local History Library. I had these photocopied, and left a set for my successors. The story, which was beginning to unveil itself, was remarkable, complex and unusual. I wrote a first draft of the book while I was at Worcester, but there was not time to complete it. So when I retired, I took to the task with renewed vigour. In this process many new papers and archives emerged. In the process of writing, a second theme emerged. What makes a place into a place? What makes up local identity and ethos? This fascinated me, not least because Tong was a small enough place to examine the matter in microcosm.

This led me in new directions. A second draft of the book emerged, incorporating this new theme. However, when I sent the document for comment to some advisors, they thought that this material detracted from the main story. Now, I have redrafted the material, so that Chapters 1 to 13 tell the story and the Epilogue now contains most of my reflections on this matter. I hope that I have said enough for others to think more about "Place" and to ask (in the title of Lucy Leppard's book) *"What is the Lure of the Local?"* In an age of globalisation, there is a danger of people losing their roots. The chief value of history is that it helps us to see where we have come from, and this will condition where we are going.

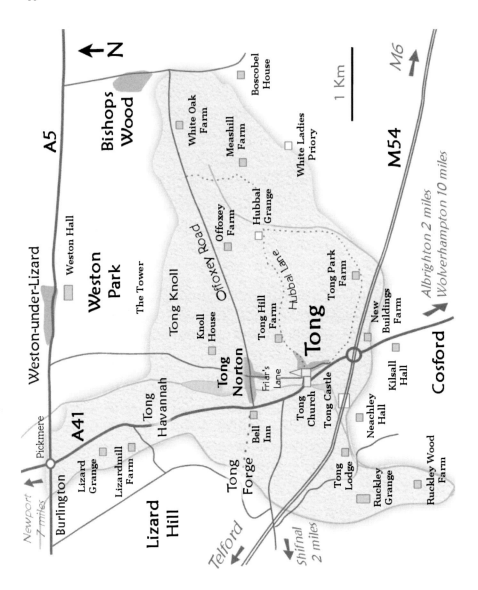

Map of the parish of Tong

(for a map of the village see page 122)

Part One: Historical Tong

Chapter 1

The Story of Tong

Nikolaus Pevsner in his **Penguin Guide to Shropshire** [1] comments that *"The great attraction of Shropshire is that it does not attract too many"*. This is true of Tong. It has been able to preserve a distinct identity, because it has not been well known. The Village encourages a deep sense of loyalty from its residents. It is not just people who shape places, but places that shape people. Places are where people meet, and stories are told. Lucy Leppard quoting Kwakiuti makes the point that *"A place is a story happening many times"*. [2] This book has collected together all the stories we can find. It tells the story of the place, and demonstrates what gives it meaning and continuity.

Tong is a slightly strange name, but it is used in other places (e.g. Kent, Yorkshire, Lancashire and Cornwall). The Domesday Book calls Tong "Tuange". The word is derived from the word 'tongue'. It is a place where there is a fork in the river, or it could be the land between two arms like tongs, or forceps. [3] There are two small rivers that meet below Ruckley Grange in the parish. [4]

Tong is situated on the Shropshire-Staffordshire border between the village of Albrighton and the old A5 road. It is just on the edge of the M54 motorway (built in 1979). The motorway has changed the landscape. Anyone turning off the motorway at exit 3, and going north on the A41, is immediately faced with Tong Church, and the village set behind it. Robert Harbison catches the flavour of the place with his comment:

"Despite a motorway nearby, the church on its mound seems to exist in a time of its own. The little village gives plenty of signs of a dignified past, fallen into disuse but not much overlaid." [5]

Any visitor discovers that the fine Church dominates the small village of about 15 houses. The rest of the parish is mainly agricultural. It has small groups of houses, spread over 12 square miles. During the second half of the twentieth century, the population has more than halved. In earlier generations, the Castle dominated the landscape and the community. But the Castle is no more.

Over the centuries, various visitors have recorded their impressions of Tong and the rest of this chapter records some of the impressions of the visitors.

During the Civil War, King Charles I marched through Tong with his army. One of the royalist soldiers, Richard Symonds, who was a great lover of Churches, gave an account in his diary:

"Satturday may 17 1645. His majestie march by Tong com Salop. A faire church, the windows much broken yet divers ancient coates of armes remaine. A faire castle neare this church called Tong Castle belonging to Pierrepoint this 18 yeares; it was the ancient seate of Stanley who came to it by marrying Vernon of the Peak at Haddon." [6]

The tombs in the Church attracted the interest of the antiquary William Dugdale, who visited Tong in September 1663. He made a detailed description of the tombs. [7]

In 1763, a Mr Coles wrote of a visit in **The Gentleman's Magazine**. As well as a description of the church, he reported:

"The Duke of Kingston's seat is at Tong Castle. The ancient College where the clergy lived is mostly demolished and what remains is partly inhabited by some poor people and partly converted into a stable." [8]

Mr Coles' visit came on the eve of great changes at Tong, caused by the arrival of George Durant (see Chapters 3 & 4). A visitor, during the Durant period, was John Byng, Lord Torrington, in 1792. He was shown round the church by the parish clerk and a farmer.

"This Church is of beautiful construction and of beautiful situation—as commanding a view of Tongue Park to the Castle and becoming a charming object from them; and a remaining wall with several arches of windows etc. With the clerk and a civil farmer I enter'd the church which is rich in monuments of antiquity, of the Stanleys and of the Vernons; as also stalls and much stained glass in the chancel; these the saints missed; tho' they spake here of Cromwell, of his cannen balls and of his attacks upon the castle. There is a small chapel of beautiful carving, that is now elegantly fitted up as a pew. There are six tuneable bells—with six handsome fellows belonging to them. I ascended a circular staircase in a pillar, with the farmer to the great bell; which weighs 50c weight, and requires three men to pull it. The bells were now chiming for church, and ought to and might have stay'd had not learned that this was the best time of seeing the castle, as the family would be to church." [9]

We see the same willingness of locals to show people round in an account of a visit in 1868 by the American Consul to Birmingham, Elihu

Burritt. Having visited Shifnal, he came to Tong late one evening, on his way to Boscobel. He and his companion stayed at the Bell Inn. They went for an evening stroll around the village:

"We found it fast asleep in the dark with scarcely a light to be seen at eight o'clock. The gate of the church was open however, and we felt our way up the walk with a staff and traced out the contour of the old Church up as far as the roof. Its windows had no speculation in its cold and silent eyes and one could hardly fancy that the departed spirits of the slumbering families entombed within those walls would wish to visit by night that still and solemn darkness. Still our nature is human in spite of philosophy and we have to confess to each other a little of the old boyhood feeling about ghosts as we put our faces to the windows and tried to recognise the objects within. After making a walk through the village without meeting a man, woman child or dog we returned to The Bell." [10]

The following morning, Burritt went to look at the recently sold Tong Castle. Then he visited the Church. He was ecstatic:

"Tong Church! Did one in five hundred of all the Americans who have visited Haddon Hall in Derbyshire ever visit this little Westminster of the Vernons? It is doubtful. It is even possible that I am the first and only American who ever saw it. Even a man well read in the general history of the country will be astonished on entering this miniature cathedral, for such it is and looks in its interior and exterior aspects. In the first place, it is doubtful if any other village or provincial church in England contains within its walls so many beautiful and costly monuments to the memory of so many noble families as this little Westminster. You see here how and when these various families intersected with each other in wedlock and interweaved the new branches they put forth as a result of the union. Here you may read their histories, their graces and virtues, if you can decipher monumental Latin." [11]

This was a terrible exaggeration, if someone has visited Bottesford, Burford, or Mells, but it demonstrates the impression the Church still makes. His description of the *"Little Westminster of the Vernons"* has been changed by local tradition into *"The Westminster Abbey of the Midlands"*. Burritt is more accurate. He then describes the tombs in detail. He admits he was able to do this because the Village schoolmaster leant him a notebook, in which he had recorded the details.

"He has collected a little history of them and deciphered and translated inscriptions which would cost even the best of scholars much time and trouble to make out". [12]

The schoolmaster took him to the Village School.

"The room was full of children, ruddy rural and happy as birds and looked as much surprised on seeing such strangers step suddenly on their perch. Our visit to this little village, which we seemed to have stumbled upon by accident was very enjoyable and gave us the satisfaction of an unexpected discovery"

Archdeacon Cranage, in his monumental survey of Shropshire churches, devotes twelve pages to Tong, and comments on the good state of the Church fabric. [13] The Revd R. W. Eyton, the author of the twelve volume **Antiquities of Shropshire** had lived in Tong as a child. In his account, he catches something of the national influence of the Lords of the Manor, but he exaggerates:

"If there be any place in Shropshire calculated alike to impress the moralist, to instruct the antiquary and interest the historian that place is Tong. It was for centuries the abode or heritage of men great either for their wisdom or their virtue, eminent from their station or their misfortunes. The retrospect of their annals alternates between the palace and the feudal castle, between the halls of Westminster and the council Chamber of princes, between the battlefield, the dungeon and the grave." [14]

The Revd J. E. Auden, as well as writing many notes and papers on Tong, gives it a key place in his **Guide to Shropshire**. [15] He devotes eleven pages to Shrewsbury, and six pages to Tong.

In 1951, John Betjeman wrote the last known description of the Castle:

"Tong Castle is now uninhabited and without roof or floors. Seen from the churchyard the landscaped park with a winding lake looks almost the size of Blenheim. The castle was remodelled in a Gothic and Moorish style in 1765 and its beauty has been impaired by the removal of domes on the corners, but enough is left to show that it was romantic and strange. The architect seems to have had in mind India and has placed at the end of the lake an obelisk designed to look from the house like the top of a Buddhist temple. The gateways and the lodge are an earnest of the house, so are other buildings in the village and the tower on Tong Knoll. The building stone is brownish gold." [16]

Betjeman's Indian speculations are entirely wrong, but he catches the romanticism of the place.

Caroline Hillier, a novelist and resident of Wolverhampton, wrote a personal account of her visit. Tong intrigued her:

"But to feel the concertina quality of time, go to Tong. There are marvellous marble monuments at Tong' a friend told me

'Oh' I said 'Marble monuments are cold and dusty; things of wet Sunday afternoons'

'But not at Tong'."

She describes the Vernon tombs, refers to Charles Dickens, and then says:

"The monuments seem most alive, as if they might smile or speak. There is no cold finality of death, I understood why the friend whose brother had recently died, had told us of this place." [17]

The most recent description of the Church is by Simon Jenkins [18]. He mainly quotes from the Church guidebook. He says that the carved Bosses are *"worthy of a cathedral"* and sums up the Church by saying that it is *"An aristocratic foundation dedicated to the memorial needs of the departed rich."*

Possibly one of nicest tributes by a visitor is that of Archdeacon Scott of Stafford. In 1898 (the year in which he died), he stayed at Tong Vicarage to write his annual Visitation Charge. Afterwards, he wrote to the Vicar:

"I cannot say how much I enjoyed my Tong sojourn. Everybody and everything was perfect and the place is a most fitting framework for such perfection. Lichfield felt so dull and void and ugly after Tong." [19]

Those who have lived in, or visited Tong, still find much to attract them.

NOTES

[1] N. Pevsner *Penguin Guide to Shropshire*

[2] L. Leppard *The Lure of the Local* p50

[3] J. Ayto & I. Crofton *Brewer's Britain & Ireland 2005* pp1115-1116 but see also *The Lore of the Land* pp632

[4] See D.H. Robinson *The Wandering Worfe*

[5] R. Harbison *England's Parish Churches* p195

[6] Symond's Diary is quoted in *Auden's Notes* vol 1. His comments on the Stanleys and Vernons are not completely accurate see Chapter 2. Symonds had been a private tutor before the Civil War and afterwards went on the Grand Tour during which he met Poussin and Caravaggio, See D. Purkiss *The English Civil War* pp359-60, 366, 567.

[7] W. Dugdale *Visitation of Shropshire* ms at Royal College of Arms. See also Dugdale's *Monasticon*.

[8] *The Gentleman's Magazine* 1763

[9] J. Byng *The Torrington Dairies*

[10] E. Burritt *Walks in the Black Country*

[11] Ibid

[12] The Schoolmaster was John Longstaff who was an antiquarian. Later, someone stole this notebook.

[13] D. H. S. Cranage *Architectural Account of the Shropshire Churches*

[14] R. W. Eyton *The Antiquities of Shropshire*

[15] J. E. Auden *The Little Red Guide to Shropshire*

[16] J. Betjeman *The Shell Guide to Shropshire*

[17] C. Hillier *A Journey to the Heart of England* pp121-3

[18] S. Jenkins *England's Thousand Best Churches* pp582-3

[19] *Tong Parish Magazine* for June 1898

View of Tong Church from the south-east (old engraving)

View of Tong Castle and Church by E. Reynolds 1823

Chapter 2
Tong Castle

There was a Roman settlement at Tong. The site of the Castle stands between the old Worcester Road and Watling Street, which is on the way to the great Roman town of Viroconium (Wroxeter). There is evidence of two Roman marching camps, established around AD47, near the river Worfe at Burlington on the northern boundary of the parish. [1]

At the time of the Norman Conquest, Tong was in the possession of Edwin, son of Alfgar, grandson of Leofric, Earl of Mercia. Following the battle of Hastings (1066), Edwin submitted to William of Normandy, who had gained the English throne. William was anxious to reward his supporters, and to secure their continuing loyalty. So Shropshire was handed over to William's cousin, Roger de Montgomery. William did this partly to keep his relatives away from London. As his tenant-in-chief, Roger was able to support the King with financial and military advice. He provided for the safety and well being of the inhabitants under his jurisdiction. The building of castles, and the founding of religious houses were effective instruments to achieve these ends. Roger held nearly 90% of the lordships and manors in Shropshire. They were mostly run by Norman tenants of Roger. He built many castles including Shrewsbury, Ludlow, Clun, Hopton, Montgomery and Oswestry.

The Domesday Book (compiled in 1086) records that Tong, with its neighbour, Donnington, were among the lands granted to Roger, who was made Earl of Shrewsbury. He had the responsibility to defend the Marches (the English-Welsh border), jointly with William fitz-Osborne the Earl of Hereford, who hold the southern portion and Hugh of Avranches, who held Cheshire.

The fertility of the soil, watered by the River Worfe, made Tong a valuable agricultural asset. [2] Prompted by the need to ensure safety for the labourers, he constructed a defensive structure. Initially, it would have been built of earth and timber, following the standard design of the many castles erected after 1066. The mound was surmounted by a wooden tower, with a flat area around and enclosed by a palisaded rampart with a surrounding a ditch. [3] Set in a fertile terrain, Tong may well have attracted marauders from less prosperous areas. In such an emergency animals would have been hustled into the castle precincts, as well as the men, women and children of the Manor.

It is possible that this first building was at Castle Hill in Tong Norton. It is mentioned in a charter dated 1185-6 but it is possible that this is the new castle built on the site where it remained until the twentieth century. Castle Hill may have been its predecessor. Over time the prosperity of the manor increased. As the population grew, these defences were, by stages, strengthened and extended; using stone instead of wood, to keep pace with the advances in the techniques of warfare. From the 12th century, most English castles were built or rebuilt in stone.

Alongside the fortifications, the erection of a Church at Tong must have made an impact on the life of the Manor. Roger had founded Shrewsbury Abbey. He joined the Benedictine Community a few days before his own death in 1094. The Church at Tong, looked after by the Shrewsbury monks, provided the population with a centre for worship. There, seasonal festivals were observed; news was shared; family events marked, and education made available to the young. So the Church complemented the Castle, as an influence in the life of the community.

Tong was just a small part of Roger's portfolio of properties. In addition to the Shropshire lands, he had estates in Sussex. There he built Arundel Castle. Also he had to attend to his affairs in Normandy. [4]

FAMILY CONNECTIONS

Another feature of post-Conquest England was: *"The close cohesion between the small group of Norman families which, between 1070 and 1087, acquired almost half the territorial wealth of England whilst retaining and increasing their recently won possessions in Normandy."* [5] The tenacity, with which Anglo-Norman families kept their estates within their own family, is shown in subsequent developments at Tong.

Roger's son, Hugh, died in 1098 and the earldom went to Robert de Belmeis. The family held Shropshire until 1167. Richard de Belmeis was Lord of the Marches, and Bishop of London, as was his nephew, also Richard. His brother, Philip, brought another religious community, the Arosian order to Tong Lizard from Dorchester Abbey. It subsequently moved to Lilleshall Abbey in 1145. Through marriage, the Belmeises were succeeded by the la Zouches. They further enlarged the Castle and built up the defences. During this period, King John confiscated the Manor, but it was finally returned to the la Zouche family. Alice la Zouche married

William de Harcourt and their daughter married Henry de Pembrugge in 1267.

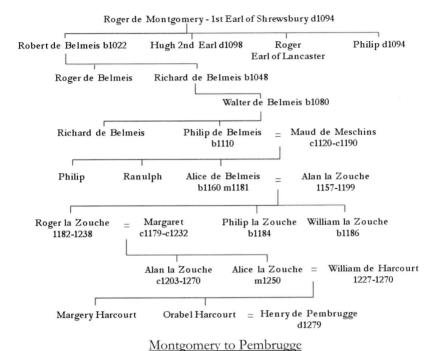

Montgomery to Pembrugge

THE PEMBRUGGES AND TONG COLLEGE

When the Pembrugge line inherited Tong, the Castle became more of a domestic centre. In the reign of Richard II (1377-1400), Fulke de Pembrugge IV obtained a license from the king to fortify Tong Castle and made it more like its sister Castle at Stokesay. His first wife Margaret Trussell had previously been married to Nicholas de Whyston who was part owner of Weston under Lizard. She was the daughter of Sir Willam Trussell and died childless in 1399, leaving as her heir William Trussell (the grandson of her uncle), then aged 14. Fulke then married Isabel Lingen, a cousin of his, who had been married twice before. One result was the founding of Tong College (see Chapter 6).

Fulke IV's sister was Juliana, who was the widow of Sir Richard Vernon of Harlaston. His heir, also called Richard, was married to Benedicta de Ludlow (died 1444). She was a daughter of Isabel de Pembrugge by her previous marriage to Sir John Ludlow. So began the Vernon occupation of Tong.

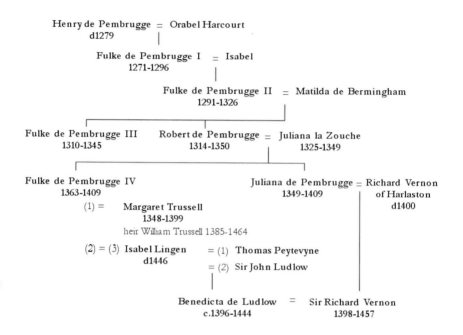

Pembrugge to Vernon

THE VERNONS AT TONG

Sir Richard Vernon was born in 1390 and died in 1451. He was Member of Parliament for Staffordshire in 1419, and for Derby in 1422, 1426 (when he was Speaker), and 1433. From 1445-51, he was Treasurer of Calais, (which he obtained through the patronage of the Duke of Buckingham and the Beaufort family.) Benedicta, his wife, brought into the marriage an estate at Hodnet, which had been owned by her father. Her mother, Isabel, was reputed to own 40 manors in England, including land at Lapley, just over the Staffordshire border from Tong. There was a ruthless streak to Richard Vernon. He held a large number of official positions, including deputy justiciar in South Wales; and owning manors from Westmoreland to Buckinghamshire, as well as five manors in South Wales. As a stockholder of sheep in the highly profitable wool trade, he farmed mainly in the Peak District. In 1440 some of his tenants in the Duchy of Lancaster estates there, (which he administered) complained to the Royal Council because he was making illegal imprisonments. He aligned himself with the Lancastrians, as did the Stanleys and the Talbots.

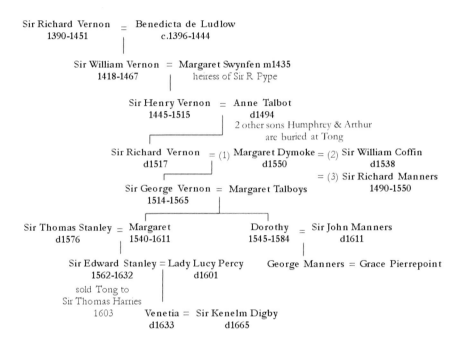

<u>Vernon to Stanley</u>

This was as nothing compared with his dealings over the Trussell estates. Sir William Trussell (1385-1464), heir to the Trussell estates, married Margery Ludlow, another daughter of Isabel de Pembrugge in 1402. This gave Fulke IV the chance to retain the estates of his first wife until his death. When William married, Fulke gave him the manor of Warmington, but persuaded him to agree that Isabel (his mother-in-law) should retain the Trussell estates in Berkshire, for a period of 20 years after Fulke IV's death. These estates included Shottesbrooke and were worth £27 p.a. In addition, Isabel retained until her death, the Trussell estates in Northamptonshire and Staffordshire worth £62 p.a.

In 1442, Richard Vernon made a claim on the Trussell estates, and he seized those in Berkshire by force. The matter went to court, and although

William Trussell was awarded damages of 120 marks, a writ of error to the King's Bench delayed payment for a long time. When Isabel died in 1446, Richard appealed against William Trussell's acquisition of the estates, and was reported to have bribed the jury. The result was that the court found in favour of Richard, on the grounds that Trussell had ousted him by force. William Trussell appealed against the verdict, but enormous damages of £2,090 were awarded to Richard Vernon. He claimed that Trussell had forged the documents. This saga was finally resolved, after the death of Richard Vernon in 1451. So William Trussell, at the age of 66, finally regained the property, which should have been his since 1402.

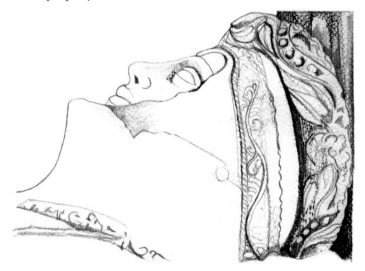

Sir Richard Vernon's Tomb

Sir Richard's second son William Vernon (1418-1467) succeeded him. He became Treasurer of Calais, and was the last person to hold for life the post of Knight Constable of England. He inherited many of his father's disputes and debts. In May 1454, he, and three other Vernons, attacked his rival William Blount and took his lands. He continued a feud with Lord Grey of Condor that led to the death of his brother, Roger, five months after his own death. William married Margaret, the daughter of William Swynfen in 1435. Her father subsequently married Alice, the widow of Sir Robert Pype and Margaret became the Pype heiress. It appears that her father also married a daughter of Sir Robert Pype by a previous marriage. [6]

Whatever the relationship, the Pype symbol is on her coat of arms. William and Margaret had five daughters and seven sons, the most important of whom was Henry Vernon.

Brass of Sir William Vernon and his wife Margaret

Henry Vernon was the most significant owner of Tong. During his tenure the Castle underwent a complete transformation. Rebuilt in red brick as a fine Tudor mansion with two wings, it was equipped with cobbled courtyards, extensive stabling and an underground tunnel that ran the whole length of the building. These features made it one of the most fashionable Shropshire buildings of the time. [7] Sir Henry made alterations to Haddon Hall at Bakewell, which he inherited from his father.

Henry married Anne Talbot, a daughter of the Earl of Shrewsbury. She died 1494. Henry made his living partly by taking on the wardship of young heirs, yet to come of age. [8] He moved in high circles. The Vernon papers at Belvoir Castle reveal Henry having correspondence with King Edward IV; the Duke of Clarence; the Earl of Warwick; King Richard III; as well as Henry VII, with whom he developed a close relationship. [9] At the battle of Bosworth, the Vernons joined with the Stanleys and the Talbots in ensuring the victory of Henry Tudor over King Richard III. Anne Talbot's brother Gilbert was also a supporter of Henry Tudor. Another of her brothers, John Talbot, lived in Albrighton, near Tong. He, with Henry Vernon, fought for Henry VII at the battle of Stoke against Lambert Simnel in 1487. It is also significant that the Talbots had supported the Vernons in their conflict with Lord Grey of Condor, some 30 years earlier.

Detail of Sir Henry Vernon's Tomb

Some of these contacts must explain why Henry Vernon became Comptroller and Treasurer to Prince Arthur in 1492. Henry was made a Knight of the Bath. (Arthur had been appointed Prince of Wales at the age of 3, in 1489.) There is some interesting correspondence from King Henry VII relating to this appointment, [10] and dating between 1492 and 1503. The first, written at Sheen on 13th April 1492, commissions Henry Vernon to start his new work on 6th May, and expressing complete trust in him. The second letter, thirteen days later, is about raising money to fight the French. A third, from Windsor in August, gives Henry Vernon full care of the Prince while the King is overseas. A letter from Sheen in June 1494 thanks Henry for his care of the Prince, and asks him to continue. Another, undated letter, summons Henry to see the King, to report on the Prince's progress. After Arthur's death, in a letter of 1503, Henry asks for Henry Vernon's help in the matter of the marriage of the King's daughter, Princess Margaret, to King James IV of Scotland, in August that year. Henry was to gather an entourage at York to escort her to Edinburgh. Another paper includes a list of people to go on this visit. It is clear that Henry remained a reliable royal servant. There is a final letter dated 30th May 1512, by which time Henry Vernon was aged 75.

Prince Arthur spent time with Henry Vernon at Haddon Hall; where there is a room known as *"The Prince's Room"*. His tutor would have been there with him. One tutor was Arthur Vernon, son of Henry, who later became Rector of Whitchurch. The Prince had several tutors. The principal tutor, appointed in 1496, was Bernard Andreas. (He was also Poet Laureate). Andreas was an Oxford graduate who was introduced to Henry VII by Bishop Fox of Winchester (1401-29). [11] Prince Arthur moved to Ludlow Castle in 1501 and Henry Vernon witnessed the marriage contract of Prince Arthur and Catherine of Aragon. The marriage took place in St Paul's Cathedral on 14th November 1501.

There is one small piece of local information, relating to this matter. In the catalogue of the books in the Tong Minister's Library [12] is listed a volume entitled ***"Summa de exemplis ac simultudinibus rerum"*** (Treatise on exemplars and similitudes) by Johannes de Sancto Geminiano. It was printed in Venice in 1499 and is a book of illustrations for use by preachers. The original was printed in Deventer in 1477. The author was a Dominican preacher, who died in 1333. The cover of the book was stamped with a Tudor rose and a pomegranate with a crown over it. This was the badge of Catherine of Aragon. The book is no longer in the library. [13] One can but speculate that Catherine left the book at Tong, while on a visit from Ludlow Castle.

Sir Henry had several children, three of them (Richard, Arthur and Humphrey) are buried at Tong. His heir was George Vernon, who was known as *"The King of the Peak"* and is buried in Bakewell Parish Church.

<u>Sir Arthur Vernon in Vernon Chantry Chapel</u>

THE STANLEYS AT TONG

George Vernon married twice. He had two daughters by his first wife. The oldest Margaret married Sir Thomas Stanley in 1558, and inherited Tong. Her younger sister, Dorothy, married John Manners and inherited Haddon Hall. Auden waxes lyrical about the myth of Dorothy Vernon's elopement and writes:

"According to the foolish and baseless fiction it was at their marriage that her sister Dorothy eloped from Haddon with John Manners, but the ballroom was not built for twenty years after the marriage, the steps not till after Dorothy's death and she was only a girl of twelve when her sister married Sir Thomas Stanley." [14]

Thomas Stanley was the second son of the Earl of Derby. John Manners was the second son of the Duke of Rutland. George Vernon died in 1565, but the Stanleys did not move to Tong for another nine years. Sir Thomas with his brother (also Edward) was involved in a plot to rescue

Mary, Queen of Scots. His arrival at Tong is recorded in a manuscript in Shrewsbury School Library:

"AD 1575 Now Lately by credible report for Sir Thomas Stanley is cum to dwell in this county and many papist gentlemen unto hym"

It is not clear what happened to Tong Castle while there were no occupants, but from this time, sporadic occupation became more of a pattern. Sir Edward Stanley, who inherited Tong, lived at different times in Lancashire, Walthamstow, and Eynsham. The lack of the constant presence of owners, at the Castle, and the subsequent neglect of the fabric, may have caused the Castle to fall into some disrepair. In 1603 Sir Edward Stanley sold Tong to Sir Thomas Harries and moved back to Eynsham.

ABSENT AND RELUCTANT OWNERS

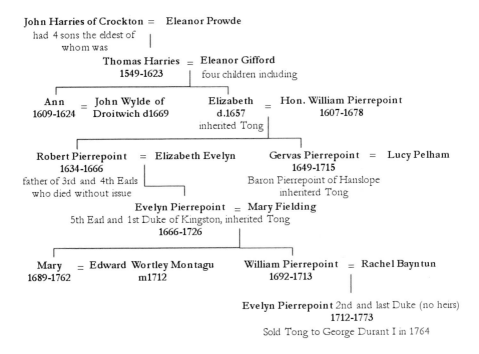

Harries to Pierrepoint

During the 100 years following the death of Henry Vernon in 1515, very little was done to maintain or repair the buildings. The marriage of Elizabeth, (2nd daughter of Sir Thomas Harries) to the Hon William Pierrepoint brought Tong into the ownership of the latter family. Pierrepoint was the second son of the first Earl of Kingston, and active in public affairs He was Sheriff of Shropshire in 1638, and MP for Great Wenlock in 1640. During the early part of the Civil War, he was one of the peace party, negotiating with King Charles I. He tried to work for peace in a way that some found inconsistent, so that Cromwell described Pierrepoint as *"my wise friend who thinks that enthroning of the king with presbytery brings spiritual slavery but with moderate episcopacy works a good peace."* [15] Although not keen on regicide, he remained in favour with Oliver Cromwell, and became a close advisor to Richard Cromwell. On the Restoration of the monarchy, he did what he could to resist and restrict the King, but retired from public life.

William's home was Holme Pierrepoint at Thoresby in Nottinghamshire. He chose to remain there during the Civil War, and was buried there. Tong Castle was involved in two sieges during the hostilities between the Royalist and Parliamentarian sides. There was some damage to the east wing of the Castle, as well as to the Church. Afterwards, William Pierrepoint arranged for repairs to be carried out, and made other alterations, (including the creation of a hanging garden). The remains of the old keep were levelled and landscaped. New features included a fountain in a pool along the western promontory, and an Italianate garden to the east of the house.

On William's death in 1678, his third son, Gervas, inherited Tong. He died without an heir in 1715, and was succeeded by his nephew Evelyn Pierrepoint, the 5th Earl and first Duke of Kingston. A prominent Whig, he was one of the leaders of fashion at the time. He was a Knight of the Garter. A brass plaque marking his stall is still in St George's Chapel Windsor. He never lived at Tong. Daniel Higgs, his agent, looked after the estate. A deed, drawn up in 1725, states: *"The Castle of Tong has been for a long time uninhabited and the park called Tong Park disparked and enclosed and there is no prospect that the said Castle will ever for the future be the residence of the Duke of Kingston and his family".*

Buck Engraving of Tong Castle at the time of the Pierrepoints about 1731

When Evelyn Pierrepoint died, his grandson, who had the same Christian name, succeeded him. He was the second (and last) Duke of Kingston. He pursued a military career, fought at the battle of Culloden, became a General in 1772, and was Lord Lieutenant for Nottinghamshire (1735-55). He died without an heir in 1773, having sold Tong in 1764.

During this period, there were a series of tenants at the Castle. These included Thomas Crump, Watkins Williams Wynne, and the Hon Henry Willoughby. When the antiquary William Cole visited Tong in 1757, the tenant was Mr. Carrington Smith *"a Roman Catholic gentleman of ancient family"*. He rented Tong until 1763.

In the summer of July 1756, Mr. Smith's brother, Walter Smythe, and his wife, Mary, stayed at the Castle. During their stay, their first daughter was born *"in the Red Room at the Castle, having arrived somewhat unexpectedly during a visit of her parents"* [16]. The midwife, who attended the birth, was Margaret Woolley of Tong. After the birth, the family went to Hampshire. When the child named Mary Anne (later known as Maria), grew up, she first married Edward Weld of Lulworth Castle in 1775. After his death, she married Thomas Fitzherbert of Swynnerton, Staffordshire. He died in 1781, leaving his widow in possession of a house in London. In 1784, Maria Fitzherbert was introduced to the Prince of Wales, later George IV. In the following year they were secretly married. Her uncle, Henry Errington, attended the wedding while Orlando Bridgeman (later Lord Bradford) kept guard at the door. This union was contrary to the Bill of Rights of 1689, and the Royal Marriage Act of 1772. In spite of this, the Prince and Mrs. Fitzherbert remained together until 1794, and again from 1799 to 1807. She lived in Brighton until her death in 1837. The birth of Maria Smythe - an episode which carried with it the germs of vicissitudes, yet to be unravelled, and typifying the culture of the age - was a prophetic harbinger of the new era about to unfold in the history of Tong Castle.

NOTES

[1] See O.S. map of Roman Britain and **Roman Camps in England** in **The Field Archaeology.**
[2] See R. W. Eyton **Antiquities of Shropshire** and also D. Robinson in **The Wandering Worfe.**
[3] A. Wharton Report of the Tong Archaeological Group
[4] H. W. C. Davis. (ed) **Regista Regnum Anglo-Normannorum** Vol 1
[5] D. C. Douglas **The Norman Achievement** p112 See also D. Carpenter **The Struggle for Mastery**
[6] In a paper on the Vernons, Professor A Cox points out that this complicated situation meant that Sir Robert Pype was Margaret's paternal grandmother's father and her maternal step-grandmother's former husband! I am grateful to Prof. Cox for his clarification of Auden's account of this period.
[7] Brick would have been stronger than the local sandstone and was used, for instance, at Hampton Court. There is evidence from the names of fields in the area that the bricks were made at Tong. See also E. Mercer **English Architecture to 1900: The Shropshire Experience.**
[8] Papers at Belvoir Castle include a document from 1495 granting Henry the wardship of the son of Robert Corbet, which he had asked for.
[9] See H. Kirke **Sir Henry Vernon of Haddon.**
[10] See an appendix to George Griffiths' **History of Tong and Boscobel** where he provides the texts of the letters as given to him by Mr. Walter de Grey Birch of the British Museum.
[11] See **Oxford Dictionary of National Biography**
[12] See Chapter 8
[13] See Auden's Notes
[14] Ibid
[15] See 11 above
[16] According to Mr. H. F. Vaughan

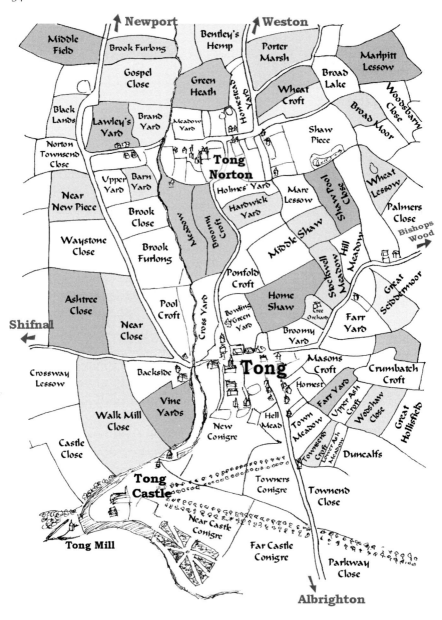

Map of Tong at the time of the Duke of Kingston (1739)

Chapter 3
George Durant Comes to Tong

"Mr Durant's offer has been shown to his Grace of Kingston and rather than break off a treaty so far advanced his grace agrees to take the £40,000, to present Mr Durant with the furniture of the new apartments, except the pictures and the tortoiseshell cabinet, the shelves and fixed presses in the Castle and the copper brewing vessels and the vessel in the cellars. The other furniture His Grace to make sale of". [1]

So reads a slightly contentious Deed of Sale, between George Durant and Evelyn Duke of Kingston in 1764. The transaction was the prelude to a huge programme of rebuilding and alterations to Tong Castle and its Estate. But who were the Durants, and how was it that George Durant came to buy Tong?

The Durant Family is traceable back to the parish of Blockley (now in Gloucestershire, then in Worcestershire) in 1544, when Henry Durant married Margaret Fletcher. From 1330, there were Durants at Barcheston in Warwickshire. Richard, the son of the above mentioned Henry, lived in Worcester from at least 1570. A house, in the Cornmarket at Worcester, still bears the words over the door ***"Love God (WB 1577 RD) Honour the King".*** The WB was William Blagdon, from whom Richard Durant (RD) purchased the land. It was from this house that the future King Charles II escaped, after the battle of Worcester in 1651.

George Durant (I) was born on 29th October, and baptised on 20th November 1732, at Hagley in Worcestershire. He was the youngest son of Josiah Durant, Rector of the Parish. His grandfather, Robert (III), had also been Rector there, and his great grandfather had been Rector of the nearby Parish of Churchill-in-Halfshire. On Josiah's death in 1764, George's elder brother John succeeded his father as Rector of Hagley; thus creating an unbroken succession of Durant incumbents in the area lasting well over 100 years. The connection with Hagley, enjoyed by generations of Durants, was due to the patronage system, giving the landowner the right to appoint the Rector of his choice, when a vacancy occurred. In Hagley, the Lyttletons, whose family seat was Hagley Hall, exercised this right in favour of the Durants. In the case of George Durant (I), however, the favour extended by the family was of an alternative nature. In 1756, having completed his studies at St Edmund's Hall Oxford, and still uncertain about what career to follow, he returned to the family home at Hagley.

Here, he found Elizabeth Lyttleton eager to enjoy his company. She was the second wife of George Lyttleton, the Chancellor of the Exchequer. They had been married in 1749, after the death of his first wife in childbirth, but they had little in common. While her husband was attending to affairs of state in London, Elizabeth remained at Hagley. George Durant soon became her regular companion, and their increasing intimacy provoked an enormous row with George Lyttleton. He threatened to divorce her. His brother commented in a letter:

"This affair has now got wind and all town talk of it; report you may suppose has exaggerated the circumstances and 'tis generally said her ladyship was caught abed with the young man... her infernal temper has left her so few friends that I don't hear of a single person who speaks in her favour, or that abuses Sir George or his family for the part he has taken. On the contrary, his enemies ascribe great merit to him for his behaviour in this delicate business". [2]

The affair must have been a great embarrassment to the Rector. Elizabeth was 16 years older that George Durant. In his diaries he calls her *"Dearest E"*. George Lyttleton forbade them to see each other, but this was ignored, and Josiah Durant was asked to send his son away. Eventually, George Lyttleton did divorce her. (He suspected that she had exchanged love letters with an Italian opera singer and flirted with a naval officer). It seems that Lyttleton thought that George Durant, as an immature young man, was sinned against by Lady Lyttleton. [3] Accordingly, he pulled some strings to get George Durant appointed as a clerk to the Pay Office in 1757.

Here, at a salary of £260 p.a., he was the lowest paid of the six officers of the Paymaster General (Henry Fox). In the following year, George Durant was appointed as Paymaster for the British troops on their expedition to Guadeloupe- a key engagement in the Seven Years War (1756-63). [4] The secretary to the Paymaster General advised a Mr Taylor not to let his son go on the voyage.

"The money is to be issued in Spanish Silver and what is more, the climate to which they are destined is not very healthy... so Durant of the Office goes."

Clearly George Lyttleton wanted him out of the way. Many people died on such trips. So George Durant left for the West Indies on 18th October 1758. Among the Durant papers are four hand-written notebooks, containing his diaries for his two expeditions. They give us a real insight into the man, and contain one of the few eyewitness accounts of the battle of Guadeloupe. Almost as soon as the ship (The "St George") sailed, they encountered very rough seas, and returned to Portsmouth, but not for long. Life on board ship was something new for George Durant. The Sunday prayer led the Rector's son to comment:

"Heard a weak sermon from a weak divine whose ignorance could equal but his impudence."

His comments make it clear he regretted going, and he is missing his *"Dearest E".* One entry describes some sort of vision involving a man who came into his cabin, stared at him, and went away. He interpreted it as a sign of Divine intervention. A flogging on the ship disturbed him greatly. He saw flying fish. When he arrived in the West Indies he met some distant relatives. He wrote letters to his father describing the state of the war, but asked him not to repeat the information, in case it turned out to be false.

During the battle of Guadeloupe, he saw people fleeing from houses and convents, and heard the great roar of the ships cannons.

"As soon as they perceived we were beginning the attack, many of the religious broke from their Convents and flew up into the mountains, the peasants drove their cattle from the shores, the Slaves removing their little Properties & the Planters raised fires along the Hills, collected all their Force & either thro' wild despair or in vain hope of terrifying our Fleet, crowded along the Shore & and in vast number pour'd into the Ports."

He reported that in the engagement, 150 troops were killed, and 200 wounded. He was appalled at the destruction, and when he landed, two days later, the whole town was deserted. The pavements were hot from burning sugar and liquor. He went into a church, not as badly destroyed as the other buildings. The description is vivid:

"It was covered with Rubbish & left in the utmost Disorder. The isles were full of Trophies & relicks, the pews were every where scattered with beads and Books; the vestries on each side of the Chancel were a foot deep in papers, prayer Books, Musick, was lights, massive Candlsticks & ten thousand nameless trinkets & all within the communion rails was crowded with those gaudy trifles which are held most sacred; so it was impossible to stir a Step without trampling on the Blessed Virgin Mary or kicking before you a wooden apostle or a maimed crucified Jesus."

Behind the church were streets that had avoided the bombardment, but had suffered from the pillaging of the soldiers and sailors. He visited the Citadel standing on a 200ft rock. The walls were six foot high and ten foot thick, with strong fortifications full of guns. He saw the carcasses of animals. He was shocked by the blood, and waste of life, not least on the ship. As he became familiar with the scene, greed got the better of him. He found a painting in a Church that he decided to steal.

"31st January. Wandered from Church to Church, saw only one Picture that I liked & made a resolution to steal it & form'd my Plot accordingly.

1st February. Cheated the centinel in the dead of night, got into the Church, scrambled up the walls brought down my Picture and carried it off without further Accident or Expence than a few broken Shins.

2nd look'd about for fresh Plunder, but found I turned Robber just in time for all the churches were turn'd into Barracks for the Negros & there was not a single thing left of Moveables, but what was unfit for everything but fuel."

He collected a bunch of letters from *"Dearest E."* from a boat that had just arrived, and then visited a prostitute.

"Made love to a French negress & found a Black at Guadeloupe & a white in Drury Lane differ'd only in Complexion, as their sentiments & winning ways seemed pretty much the same: - took my E still nearer my soul & wished the mind only could form the Body & make the person lovely, then would my dearest love be more an Angel & these impure Harbingers of Leudness be as like the brutes in Figure as in action."

There are hints of dubious financial dealings. He saved £2,331 in a deal with Barbados, by sending the coinage in weight rather than in value. He became bored because there was not enough to do. He commented on the death of the greatly disliked General Hopson, who was in command of the land Forces.

"One great comfort to me was that the Public had receiv'd no loss for a Man so Weak & obstinate so self-partial & self-interested, was never yet trust'd with so important a Command. Those who sent him have much to answer for, for it was as impolitic as it was wicked to put the lives of so many thousands into the hands of one who neither knew how to save them with credit not to let them fall with honour."

He then journeyed to St Louis, and was very ill:

"Purged excessive– full of pain– my head Splitting, my heart aking & my bladder bursting; void of all comforts, without either Strength or Spirits, bereaved of every blessing & almost lost hope! – settled all my affairs & began to think seriously & not to fear death, but too terrible for my E! At Night used fomentations & underwent several other and disagreeable Operations."

He recovered, and used his time writing letters for officers and dealing with the finances. He came home in May 1759.

In 1762, George Durant set out on a further expedition. This time it was to Havana. Henry Fox was again instrumental. He wrote to Mr Nicholl, of the Pay Office, to tell him that Durant had asked to go. On 15th Feb 1762 Fox wrote to Lord Albermarle, the commander of the expedition:

'I wish Mr Lechmere had taken his determination to decline the deputy paymastership a little earlier... The very short time he has left me has made it extremely difficult to find a proper person... I have appointed Mr Durant who is first clerk in my office, well acquainted with the business and was employed in the same capacity with the expedition of Guadeloupe. He behaved himself very well in that service. I have promised him he shall remain with the troops as long as they continue abroad; it would not have been worth his while to have undertaken on any other terms.'

The letter continues with dire warnings of the risks involved. If Durant was killed, his possessions and papers were to be kept together, until someone can replace him. A bond for £20,000 was taken out on his behalf. The expedition left in March 1762, consisting of 53 warships and 15,500 soldiers. They arrived in Martinique a month later, and in Havana on 29th June. They captured Monte Casino on 30th July. The city capitulated on 14th August, and a large amount of booty was taken. It was from this venture that George Durant returned a very rich man with over £300,000. (The equivalent today would be around £15 million)

What were the sources of such wealth? There is ample evidence that those working in the Paymaster's Office were able to make money. Peter Taylor, who was Paymaster in Germany at the same time, made a personal profit of £400,000. The matter was examined by T. H. McGuffie. [5] There is a reference in the family papers to an enquiry into George Durant's handling of the accounts, suggesting that the matter was not straightforward. His first trip had given him ideas for a lucrative future. He was able to implement them on his second visit. McGuffie offers four possible opportunities:

1. Buying and selling coinage at different rates of exchange and keeping the difference.

2. Henry Fox's account for the Havana expedition reveals that there was a surplus of surreptitious income. Durant gained his own spoils. (A list of the contents of Tong Castle in 1786 included among the paintings

"Twelve Saints full length brought from Havana" and the painting stolen from the Church is still extant.

3. To pay for the expedition, Durant was given £271.17s and 3 pence. To balance this, there are 38 payments of bills, some for very large amounts, but the Balance books do not exist. He may have been able to pay himself quite a bit.

4. There was considerable Prize Money to be made from the Sack of Havana – over £736,000. The commanders (Pocock and Albermarle) had 5/15th between them and they agreed to distribute 1/15th between two deputy commanders, and of the remaining 9/15th half should go to the Navy, and half to the land forces. The Army share amounted to £221,000. This would give the privates £4. 1s and half pence. But of the 12,000 troops only 1,485 survived (5,000 died from sickness). If Durant had kept the difference for himself, that alone would have yielded over £30,000.

There was probably a further source of income. The Durant papers contain references that imply participation in the Slave Trade. There is one document referring to a list of slaves. Another mentions an argument between Major Charnock Payne (who had been in the West Indies with Durant, and later married his widow) and the Revd Charles Buckeridge (George Durant's cousin, who became Vicar of Tong in 1791). The document is partly about the payment of Mr Buckeridge, but it also refers to papers to be destroyed, as well as subject not to be mentioned in the future. Suffice it to say that the Anti-Slavery campaign was in progress from 1787. It is also significant that the Telephone Directory of one Island of the Windward Islands reveals that almost everybody is named *"Durant"*. Slaves took the name of their owner. There can be little doubt that George Durant profited from the lucrative traffic in slaves.

On his return in 1763, George Durant found himself with the means to purchase a substantial property. We have already seen that the Pierrepoints were anxious to dispose of Tong. There is a correspondence between Walter Stubbs of Tong and the Duke of Kingston's agent, Mr Sherring at Thoresby. In May 1761, he wrote to say that he was frustrated in getting a positive response from Mr Bridgeman of Weston to purchase the estate. Mr Sherring then commissioned a full valuation of the entire estate, which was completed on 5th May 1763 [6]. This listed the present valuation (see Appendix C), present rent, and potential new rent as a means of providing a full valuation.

Then on 3rd October 1763, Mr Stubbs reported a new development. Mr Bridgeman might still purchase, if he inherits Weston, to enlarge the estate, but continued:

"We have had a gentleman viewing the Tong Estate last week. He dined 2 days in Tong and he called at my house but I happened to be from home and he wanted me to show him a map of it and how many acres the estate was. I sent note by Tildesley that you had all the survey and plans in your hands which you took away with you when you left last Tuesday. They call the gentleman Durant. I suppose this is the same person you mentioned."

Stubbs had been checking the inventory on the contents of Tong Castle and had found a Pewter Chamber pot missing. But Mr Carrington Smith was still is residence, and Stubbs needed to know when to collect the rent from Smith, who would be leaving. The furniture in the Castle had to be valued. Durant was given the valuations of the whole estate, and he appointed a solicitor in Wolverhampton to act on his behalf. Then, he contested the valuation, and he asked for anther one to be drawn up by an independent valuer. The difference in the two valuations turned out to be £60. 1s 6d per annum, this being £1,800 on a 30 year lease. Durant argued that the asking price of £45,600 should be reduced to £42,680. But he went further; he let it be known that he had been offered another estate in Buckinghamshire and commented:

"The Castle and the grounds are in a miserable state of repair. The rain is coming in through the leads and in need of reroofing."

Similarly the walled garden was collapsing, and many of the farms were in a poor state with broken fences. Some had not been occupied for a long time. Other correspondence revealed the truth of this and the fact that the wall of the mill had fallen down. It was clear that running Tong from Thoresby had not really worked.

After this rather difficult negotiation, the whole estate was sold on a 30-year lease (which was subsequently renewed twice) for £40,000. Durant embarked on the process of restoring the Castle, and developing the estate, in a way that changed it forever. In 1765, he had designs for the landscape, and probably the Castle, made by Capability Brown. Brown knew the area, as he had previously done work at Weston Park and at Chillington. It looks as if Brown only made one visit. His account book states, *"To various plans and elevations made for Tong Castle and for the journey's there £52.10s"* which was his normal charge for outline plans. [7]

The work on the Castle was vast. It was built around the foundations of the 16th century Castle Cellars and underground passages were added and well as other rooms. (When a surveyor looked at the property in 1855, he recommended that it should be demolished because the foundations were inadequate for the structure erected above). A new stable block was built, as well as an Ice House. [8]

There are many pictures of the Castle, with its turrets, in what was called "The Moroccan Style". Many details about the interior are given in two documents. The first is a description of the house and its contents from 1789; and the second is the sale catalogue of 1855. There were two wine vaults to hold 460 dozen bottles of wine; an ale cellar holding 40 hogsheads; and stabling for 18 horses with a Coach House for four carriages. The 1789 catalogue contains a description of each room, its contents and pictures. The rooms are all named: two Dining Rooms, a Winter Drawing Room, Breakfast Parlour and a Saloon on the ground floor. (See illustation on page 48). On the first floor, reached by a grand staircase, were a Green and a Gold Room; two libraries; Dressing Room; the Crimson Bedroom; the Bamboo Room (containing a bamboo bed), a Long Gallery; Straw Coloured Room; Chintz Room (containing a curious Lava slab); a Music Room (with an organ), and various dressing rooms. On the top floor were six more bedrooms; a Billiard Room; six garret rooms for servants and several other rooms, still unfinished in 1855. The cellars contained the kitchens, Butler's pantry and servants quarters. This was typical of the sort of housing being built at that period by newcomers trying to make an impact among the country gentry. [9]

The list of 228 paintings include works by Rubens, van Dyke, Kneller, Lely, Rembrandt, Reynolds (including portraits of Josiah Durant and his son), Titian, Poussin, Vandevelde, Holbein, Delsarto, Durer, Tintoretto and Verrio. It is not possible to tell how many were copies. There were also some sculptures. In 1841, there were eleven female servants, three male servants, and an artist living in the Castle. In addition, employees included gardeners, gamekeepers, and others living in houses on the estate.

Tong Castle the seat of Benjamin Charnock Payne print of 1789

The landscaping had been a major part of Capability Brown's advice. Dr Robinson gives a short summary:

"Brown built a big dam across the narrow valley, very close to the castle and dug out much of the soil on the meadow. In this way he created a long narrow crescent of a lake almost 1,400 yards long from Castle to Castle Hill crossed not far from the Church by the highway from Tong to Newport. The part nearer the castle became known as Church Pool or North pool while the upper part was called Castle Hill Pool". [10]

Later, the level of the Old Mill dam, situated 100 yards below the newly constructed dam, was raised, close to the Castle. This caused Kilsall brook to swell out into another piece of water, known as the South Pool. This became the subject of litigation between Mr. Bishton of Kilsall and George Durant. It was done without any consultation, and George Durant ended up in court in 1775 for digging a pool across the highway.

Thus we see the Castle set amidst an elaborate landscape, within its own domain. When Torrington visited in 1792, he was appalled by it:

"This place purchas'd by Mr D- has been rebuilt in a most overgrown taste; and would require a very large fortune to keep up. How people can build such pompous edifices

with out a sufficiency of surrounding estate is wonderful! And yet how commonly it is done. Vanity easily triumphs over reason; it impoverishes the first and now ruins succeeding generations. And how a tenant can be found is surprising– to ramble about such an edifice- instead of the quiet cheapness of a smaller house!

It is a grand and beautiful place; attended by the housekeeper I surveyed the house; the staircase is very fine, the rooms well sized and well furnished; the bedchambers excellent; there is on the first floor a vast musick room but no library! Your hasty wealth thinks not of that- every part of this magnificent house is covered by pictures– from cities and other auctions of dying Saints, naked Venuses and drunken Bacchanalls. Now why all this offensive shew; disgusting to every English eye that has not been harden'd in Italy – Surely the intention of paintings was the cheer the mind, and restore your pleasures; to survey your ancestry with conscious esteem; to view the beauties of nature; – to restore your pleasures; to survey your ancestry with conscious esteem; to view the beauties of nature; – to restore the memories of famous horses, and of faithful dogs; – but why produce savage and indecent exhibitions, before your child's eyes? Why is Ovid's Metamorphosis to be produced in full display? Why are the glorious feasts of Jupiter to be held before our eyes and why are we to be encouraged by satyrs to peep at naked sleeping beauty? Now with all this to shew, the first of comforts was wanting, some good fires." [11]

He makes a prophetic statement about the future:

"This would be a grand place: as it is, some West Indians [12] may hire it for a few years; but if once deserted, these houses soon tumble to pieces."

George Durant also had political ambitions. He stood in a Southwark bye-election in September 1763, but was not elected. His contact for this was Mark Beaufoy of Southwark, and, with his help, he stood to be MP for Evesham. In September 1767 Beaufoy wrote to Sir John Rushout who, with his son, were the sitting MPs of the constituency:

"Having been informed by letters from Evesham of thy resolution not to stand a contested election for that borough, I take liberty on behalf of Mr Durant to renew my proposal when I had the pleasure of waiting upon thee at Norwich, viz. That in consideration of thy interest Mr Durant will pay the expense of Mr Rushout's return provided Mr Durant becomes one of the sitting members"

There are further references to Durant spending money to gain this seat. At the election in 1768, he and Mr Rushout were elected. There is little sign of him being active in Parliament. He voted for the expulsion of Wilkes in 1769. An MP until 1774, he stood as a Tory, at a time when the Whig ascendancy was coming to an end.

He needed a London house. He purchased a site on the north side of Portman Square, and built a town house there in 1768. Selling it in 1771, he moved to New Palace Yard, where he had lived, while at the Pay Office. This house remained his London address until he died.

By this time *"Dearest E"* had vanished from the scene, but there were other amorous affairs. The chief of these was Elizabeth Hamilton, who lived in London. There were two children of this union, George, born in 1770, and Henry, born in 1774 (the year after his father's marriage). George Hamilton became a civil servant, and worked in the Stamps Office in Dublin. When he died in 1832, his half brother George Durant (II) erected a memorial tablet to him in the grounds of Tong Castle. Henry became Governor of Accra, and died in 1808. Elizabeth and her two sons were left annuities in George Durant's will.

George Durant was 41 when he married. His marriage was the result of his political manoeuvrings. Maria was the daughter of Mark Beaufoy, who had helped him to get elected. Beaufoy had been born in Evesham, but became a vinegar brewer at Cupar Gardens in Southwark. His did not approve of the marriage. ***The Gentleman's Magazine*** commented:

> *"As she was a Quaker born and bred, Mark Beaufoy would not consent to the marriage, Maria was born in Cupar Gardens, Lambeth. She went up to Edinburgh with her cousin William Biddle and his wife Sarah and married George Durant there. They then went on a tour of Scotland where Dr Johnson and Boswell met them at a remote Inn where all the travellers had to share a bedroom. Boswell says it caused acute embarrassment to the 'young bride a Mrs Durant'."* [13]

The elopement took place in 1773. With this background, it is understandable that there was strong disagreement, later, over the Beaufoy money, in connection with the Durant estate. Being a Quaker, Maria had not been baptised, so when they arrived, she was baptised in Tong Church. There were two children of this marriage. George Durant (II) was born in 1776, and baptised at St Margaret's Westminster. A daughter, Maria, was born in 1779, and died aged 4. George Durant (I) died (aged 47) on 4th August 1780 and was buried in Tong Church on 16th August. His widow was very bereft. Her father wrote to her brother:

> *"thy sister does not recover her spirits, neither will she I believe whilst she continues at the castle, for every night, after dark she goes to the church porch and spends some time giving vent to her grief, and all that we can say does not divert her from it."* [14]

When her husband died, she was only 25. George's Will, made at the last minute, was in two sections bearing the dates 3rd and 4th August. There was a strong provision for his wife and family, and legacies to some servants. There was a complex arrangement for the succession in relation to the estate. The guardians of his children were his wife and Mr Benjamin Charnock Payne. He had been a Major in the 99th Regiment of Foot, which had been raised in Jamaica for the Havana expedition. One account book implies that Durant owed him money.

This joint guardianship brought Maria and Charnock Payne together, and they were married at St. James' Piccadilly in January 1783. He was living in Charlotte Street, Bloomsbury. They had a daughter, who was baptised at St George's Bloomsbury in June 1784. There are hints that they may have tried to sell Tong. A catalogue, drawn up like a sale catalogue, was produced in 1789. It could have been used for visitors or to attract tenants, equally it may have been produced in an attempt at a sale. The first 30-year lease would have been up in 1794, thus giving a few years to facilitate a sale. When Torrington visited in 1792, the Plowden family rented the Castle. There is also a print of Tong Castle, dated 1789 under which is written *"The seat of Benjamin Charnock Payne Esq."*. He died in 1793. Mrs Payne then married a Col Chapman, and they went to live in Dawlish, where she died in 1832. Her son did not allow her to be buried at Tong. In the family, she was always referred to as *"Mrs Chapman"*.

NOTES

[1] I am grateful to Lady Higgs for access to the Durant papers. Much of this Chapter and next are derived from these papers and also to work done by James Bath, (a Durant descendent of Sydney, Australia). His findings are published in **Durant of Worcester and Tong: A Family History 1998**. See also the transcription of George Durant's Diaries Ed Alan J Guy in **George Durant's Journal of the Expedition to Martinique and Guadalupe October 1758-May 1759.** Army Records Society 1997

[2] Quoted in J. Bath

[3] Not that Lyttleton had a high view of marriage. He once wrote: *"Marriage must be considered as a species of traffic and as much a matter of commerce as any commodity that fills the warehouse of a merchant…One marries for connections, another for wealth, a third for lust, a fourth to have an heir, to oblige his parents and so on."* See Blunt and Wyndahm **Thomas Lord Lyttleton.**

[4] For the Seven Years War see F. Anderson **Crucible of War. The Seven Years War and the Fate of the Empire in British North America 1754-1766.**

[5] T. H. McGuffie *A Deputy Paymaster's Fortune* in the *Journal of the Society for Army Historical Research*.

[6] The details are from Manvers Papers from Thoresby, deposited in Nottingham University Library.

[7] Paul Stamper essay *"Of Naked Venuses and Drunken Bacchanals: The Durants of Tong Castle"*

[8] Now at the Avoncroft Museum of Buildings in Bromsgrove.

[9] See L. Stone *An Open Elite* pp207ff

[10] See D. H. Robinson *The Wandering Worfe* pp50-54

[11] J. Byng *The Torrington Diaries 1781-94*. He was wrong about the library -his memory must have tricked him.

[12] By the word "West Indians" he meant English people, who had been fortune hunters in the West Indies.

[13] *The Gentleman's Magazine*

[14] Quoted in G. Beaufoy *Leaves from a Beech Tree*

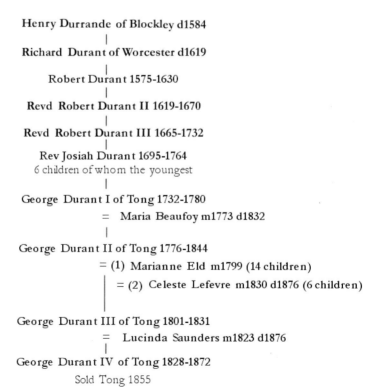

Henry Durrande of Blockley d1584
|
Richard Durant of Worcester d1619
|
Robert Durant 1575-1630
|
Revd Robert Durant II 1619-1670
|
Revd Robert Durant III 1665-1732
|
Rev Josiah Durant 1695-1764
6 children of whom the youngest
|
George Durant I of Tong 1732-1780
= Maria Beaufoy m1773 d1832
|
George Durant II of Tong 1776-1844
= (1) Marianne Eld m1799 (14 children)
= (2) Celeste Lefevre m1830 d1876 (6 children)

George Durant III of Tong 1801-1831
= Lucinda Saunders m1823 d1876
|
George Durant IV of Tong 1828-1872
Sold Tong 1855

Durant Family Tree

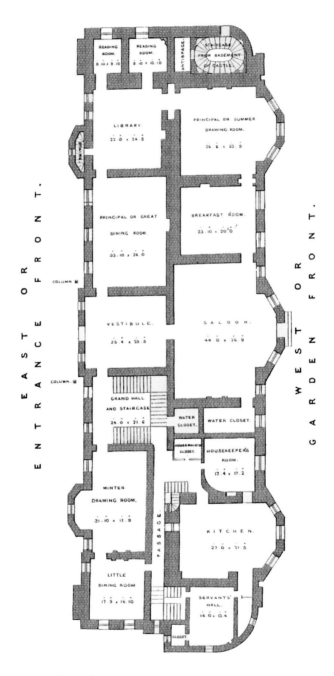

Plan of the ground floor of Tong Castle

Chapter 4

"Beati Qui Durant"

In 1797, when he was 21, George Durant (II) inherited the Tong Estate. For a short time, he had been educated at a small school in nearby Brewood. When his mother, Mrs Payne, moved to London he went to school in Paddington for a year, and then to Charterhouse. He attended Worcester College Oxford, leaving in 1794. He joined the Staffordshire Militia in 1797. In the following year, he was with the militia in Winchester, as part of the preparation for the threatened Napoleonic invasion. In 1804 he became a major in the Shropshire Militia; was appointed a Justice of the Peace and in 1813 became a Deputy Lieutenant for Shropshire. He was a Freemason. All this was typical of a newcomer trying to make his mark in county society. In 1799 he married Marrianne Eld of Seighford. He left an indelible mark on Tong, but we need to begin with his personal and family life. This was summarised, with amazing frankness, by **The Shrewsbury Chronicle**, in his obituary:

"In 1799 Col Durant married Marrianne daughter of Francis Eld of Seighford Hall in the County of Stafford by whom he had issue 14 children, eight of whom have since died. It is with great reluctance that we approach this part of Mr Durant's life.

Highly educated of great natural abilities, and possessed of those intrinsic qualities which caused his society to be courted in public; yet his domestic circle was far from being the happy home it ought to have been. Although blessed with an amiable wife and family of children any gentleman might be proud of, he like the fallen Majesty of Denmark left the royal feast to prey on garbage. In fact his illicit amours were carried on so undisguisedly that it was impossible for them not to reach the ears of Mrs Durant and her remonstrances being answered by harsh treatment, at length she was obliged to quit her magnificent but unhappy abode and seek the shelter of her parental roof where she was received kindly by him who has so long been venerated as a real old English Gentleman." [1]

Before he started his illicit affairs, George Durant (II) had a child every year. By 1808, his wife knew what was going on. Mary Jane Bradbury came to the Castle, as a nursemaid in 1807, and was the mother of three of his children to whom he gave the surname "St George' (the name of the ship on which his father had gone to the West Indies). The first child was born in 1808. Mrs Durant was so upset that she went home to her father. This led George to write a grovelling letter to her brother:

"My Dear Sir,

I am again most obliged to write to you in my distress; I am the most wretched man alive; my poor dear Marrianne has behaved like an angel, but it is impossible that she can ever forgive me. On Friday last she heard of the brutal passion which had hurried me to commit what I shall ever repent to my last hour. One of the women confessed to her that I had been criminally connected to her. As I might have expected she insisted on leaving the house instantly, the carriage took her on the road to London; but as I could never bear the idea of parting from her, I followed it on horseback, and she most indulgently consented to return. I cannot object to the present determination of being sometime in Seighford, as I hope she will recover the tranquillity I have so miserably destroyed: would she but once consent to return here I would relinquish everything in the world to her guidance, and if ever I prove ungrateful for her kindness would willingly live on bread and water to give her possession of all my property. Your kindness will, I am assured, send me an answer by my servant and I hope bring her leave to come to Seighford to fetch her home. I trust nothing will induce you to let her leave Seighford, as I know she would rather suffer poverty than let her family know where she retired to, and in her present disposition I fear she might make away with herself". [2]

She did return, but made it a legal condition that he set aside money, if she chose to live separately. But George's habits did not change, and, in

1809 he had a child by another servant, Elizabeth Cliffe. The next year, Mary Bradbury had a second child. Marrianne left again, and she agreed to return only if they went to live in Devon. After some time there, they moved to Bath. During this time, his wife had two more children. Then George returned to Tong, and his wife went to live in London. Finally, she was forced to return to Tong, because she had no money and was expecting twins. They were born in September 1811. In December 1811, Mary Bradbury had a third child.

In 1815, the Durants went on a trip to Paris for two weeks. In 1817, while she was staying with her father, Mrs Durant was accused by her husband of having had an affair with the children's tutor. She returned to refute the charge, but after a few days, she was thrown out of the house. She then insisted that the settlement, agreed earlier, should be implemented. However, it did not stand up in law, and so she instigated divorce proceedings.

The case, in the Ecclesiastical Court, lasted from 1820 to 1825. George Durant employed a dubious lawyer, who used considerable delaying tactics, and was sporadically 'ill' for several months at a time. The charges laid against George Durant were as follows:

"Mr Durant is charged with having formed in 1807 an adulterous connection with Mary Bradbury, and having had three children by her… and he is alleged to have acknowledged and supported these children. He is also charged with having formed another adulterous connection with Elizabeth Cliffe by whom he had a child born on 19th June 1809, both these persons were nursery maids in his family. In 1816 he is charged with an adulterous connection with Mary Dyke, his dairymaid; of that connection no child was born which he acknowledged. It is alleged that in June 1816 he was seen with her in the criminal act. In 1818 he is charged with adulterous connection with Jane James, a labourer's wife, of the same family and on 26th April 1820, it is asserted that he was caught in the act in a room in her cottage called White Oak Lodge." [3]

There were various witnesses to some of these events. When the liaison began, Mary Bradbury was only 15. Having come to work at the Castle in May 1807, she left, pregnant, 18 months later. The Court proceedings reveal how Durant used every opportunity to seduce her. The prosecuting lawyer put it like this:

"This the mode in which this father of a family seduces this poor girl, the attendant upon his own children– almost a child herself; and these are the sort of places where he carried on his criminal intercourse– in a brew house, laundry or unfurnished apartment

adjoining the stables, watching when other servants were out of the way. I agree with what was said in the argument that this wholly takes off the improbability that he was connected with his dairymaid in the fowl yard or shrubbery; or with labourer's wives on the floors of their own cottages."

The affair, with Elizabeth Cliffe, took place while Mary Bradbury was pregnant. Once, while Mrs Durant was away, he was found in bed with Cliffe in the room opposite the Nursery. The servants were shocked, and pulled him away from her saying that he was *"always after her"*. This conduct, said the lawyer was *"more immoral, more degrading and more disgraceful– making a brothel of his own house…. Scarcely disguising his guilt from his servants"*

In the end, Mrs Durant was granted a divorce and alimony of £600 p.a. The solicitor contested the amount of the alimony, and after two years' negotiations, it was reduced to £400. To celebrate this achievement, George Durant built a monument on Knoll Hill. It was a square building, two stories high, surmounted by pillars 80ft high. A stone over the door was inscribed with the words **"Optimo Adico TW"** (TW was the solicitor, who ended up in jail on other offences).

Following the divorce, George Durant moved to Paris with his daughters and younger sons. He purchased a Villa called *"Rosscotte"* at Clamarte. At Rennes, he met the twenty year old Marie Celeste Lefevre. He described it as *"love at first sight"*; and she became governess to his children. Durant's carriage in Paris had the Durant coat of arms, with the Fleur de Lys, on it. This was also the French royal emblem, and it gave him social status. One daughter died. She is buried in Pierre Lachaisse cemetery. [4]

Mrs Durant died at Seighford, aged 48, in April 1829. (However there is no remaining memorial to her at Seighford.) So George returned to Tong. He married Celeste, in Tong Church, on 25th September 1830. He was 54 and she was 29. She did not like Tong very much, but, for her benefit, he imported edible snails and frogs. They bought a house in Camden Terrace in London, and later moved to Hyde Park Gate. In 1834, he purchased Childwick Hall, an estate of 87 acres, near St Albans. [5] It looks as if he may have decided to move there. Hertfordshire was a popular place for people who spent time in London. In 1833, a Lady Rose offered him £500 p.a. to rent Tong, but the offer was withdrawn.

George Durant was reputed to have a child in every cottage on the Tong estate. He liked to be godfather to them, and gave them strange names like *"Napoleon Wedge"*, *"Columbine Cherrington"*, *"Gustavus Adolphus Martin"*,

"Luther Martin" and *"Cinderella Greatback"*. It is almost as if he saw these children as playthings.

The three sons of Mary Bradbury (Edwin, George and Leonard Henry) lived with her in Wolverhampton but their father paid for their education. He called them by the surname *"St George"*. His legitimate sons refused to do this, and called them 'Bradbury' to upset their father. Edwin and George trained as doctors in London. Leonard Henry want to St David's College Lampeter, and trained for the priesthood. He was ordained in 1838 to a curacy in Presteigne. When priested, he became curate at Tong. In 1839, his father appointed him as vicar. Leonard spent two of his four years, as incumbent, living in France. He left in 1843, preaching his final sermon on the text *"Is thine eye evil because I am good?"* (Matthew 20 v18).

His appointment may have been made to save money. When the previous curate left, George Durant asked the Bishop if he could use the stipend income to pay a curate, because the incumbent (Dr Mucklestone) was incapable. The Bishop replied that it was up to Dr Mucklestone. When this elderly incumbent retired in a confused state of mind, he left an unpaid dilapidations bill of £115. His son, who was a Priest Vicar at Lichfield Cathedral, wrote to the Bishop saying he thought this was unfair:

"Now as the resignation of the living is likely to be advantageous to Mr Durant, who I understand presented his son for it. I cannot but think that my father has been harshly dealt with in the exaction of so large a sum."

The Bishop responded by sending an anonymous £200, through a third party stating *"I think it will take away every unpleasant feeling of obligations if they remain ignorant from whom the aid comes."* [6] So Durant got the money.

At this time, a major incident took place, which sums up the state of family relationships and reveals the underlying issues. On 18th June 1839, George Durant (II) wrote to the Bishop's Legal Officer at Lichfield accusing two of his sons of defamation of character. He stated that, after he remarried, the sons of his first marriage turned against him:

"On the 9th June Ernest and Anguish came into my yard with six dogs and beat my yard dog (a scotch terrier) to death while their mastiffs held him down. They presented to claim access by a road through the yard which has been legally stopped for 26 years.

Ernest Durant has married a solicitor's widow and he is in a cottage adjoining my land where he increasingly has chimney fires and is firing guns by my poolside and insulting members of my family whenever they are in sight. Please to say immediately how to proceed." [7]

Durant enclosed a set of signed witness statements. One is from George St George; two are from the village constable and a police officer; and the others are by servants. It is clear this was the culmination of a series of events instigated by Ernest and Anguish, asserting their rights to walk through the stable yard. Twice on previous days the village constable had been called to prevent it. But the real causes were deeper. On the 9th June they broke down the fence and came in with six dogs, three servants and a brace of pistols each. The disturbance bought the family out onto the balcony. The party included, George, the second Mrs Durant, their neighbour Mrs Bishton, George St George and Leonard Henry who had just become incumbent. Ernest shouted up to his stepmother *"Get in you decayed, grey faced and grey headed old villainous scoundrel"* and then said to her *"You infernal whore. Damn your catholic soul. May hell soon find your damned soul. Damn you, you Bloody bitch"*. He then turned on his father *"You are a murderer– You gave my mother venereal disease five times"*. So the resentment of years finally burst out.

With Mr Durant's agreement, the Bishop's Legal Officer wrote to Ernest, inviting him to send a written public apology. (The Civil Courts would deal with the matter of the fence and the dog.) On 25th June, Ernest replied refusing to apologise. He asserted that he had a right of way, and went on to say that the accusations of being a whore were not addressed to Celeste, but to Mary Bradbury. The final letter in the correspondence is from George Durant on 3rd July dropping the whole case. It is easy to see why. The accusation about venereal disease was almost certainly true. Marianne had died at the young age of 48. If it went to court all this would become public.

This explains the events of the following year, when George St George was taken to court in Shrewsbury for shooting Ernest Durant. The charge was finally reduced to *"attempting to discharge a loaded pistol"*. (We need to remember that his father was a J.P.) Another brawl with Bruce Durant led to George St George being imprisoned in Shrewsbury for 18 months. In 1841, he left for New Zealand. He settled in New Plymouth, established a medical practice and married one of his fellow passengers. He became the first doctor to the Maoris, and also practised as a chemist. In March 1842, Durant recorded in his diary *"Had a letter from poor George in New Zealand who is very well and happy"*. That year his brother, Edwin, joined him as a business partner.

George and Celeste divided their time between London and Tong. Between 1832-7 they were mainly in London. Happily, we have George's diaries for most of the period, giving us many insights into their family life. They had six children, four of whom died in infancy. In the grounds of the Castle there was a wooden hut with a black interior on which were painted luminous demons. When the children misbehaved, they were locked in it. Their son, Mark, died at the age of seven because his father insisted that he should learn to swim, and threw him, fully clothed, into the Castle Pool and was drowned. His burial took place at midnight, with a torchlight procession to the Church.

There were endless family rows with Ernest and Frank. Once, Ernest built a gallows with an effigy of his father on it. There was much illness and death to cope with, both of children and dogs. George Durant reveals himself as a compassionate man, trying endless remedies for his suffering wife and children. A baby called Cecil was born on 8th September 1831 but was never well. The diary entry for 19th March 1832 reads *"Poor dear Cecil very ill and screamed violently all night. Mr Crump came and gave him a very large dose of laudanum to make him die easily."*

Following this event, the family went on holiday to Liverpool for eight weeks. Maria was often ill, and in 1832 was sent to Leamington to convalesce. In September that year he wrote *"Maria not unwell for the first time"* but six month later, she had relapsed, and died in Kensington. Her body was sent to Tong for burial.

There was another sad event in 1833. The dairy contains this entry:

"Celeste was delivered of a female child who I have no doubt was strangled at birth. It came out with its feet first and I saw them move but she was dead ten minutes before the head came out. The midwife denies it came out feet first. She certainly killed the little girl but it was very small for 7 months, as Celeste calculated, but the hair which I kept was fine and the nails and hands quite perfect… Mr Dean made a neat coffin was we took it to be buried in Chrysom's cemetery at 11 at night." [8]

In 1838 their daughter, Rose, was so ill that they consulted a leading surgeon, Sir Astley Cooper, who described the case as *"most alarming and proceeded from water on the brain"*. She became hysterical and died on 24th March. Durant wrote *"Rose took a fainting fit in the afternoon – Revd Mr Woodhouse gave her the sacrament – my precious dear affectionate child died half past 5 p.m. She took a most affectionate leave of everybody and wishes Ed and Eliz and their child safe over the sea"*. [9]

The Diaries give some signs of social life. There were visits by relatives– not always welcome. Celeste's mother once arrived in the middle of the night, having walked from Shifnal station, pushing her luggage in a barrow. There was an occasional dinner party, and a trip to hear Paganini in Birmingham.

They attended Church every Sunday. When in London, he went to Brompton or Kensington Parish Church. Celeste attended a Roman Catholic Church, and had several of her children baptised as Catholics. At

Tong, Durant turned the Chantry Chapel into his family pew. The walls were panelled, and it had settees and a fireplace. Halfway through the morning service, a servant came up from the Castle with a donkey carrying Mr Durant's lunch. The servant carried the tray down through the Church into the Chapel. Every Sunday, after the vicar left, he catechised the children. Each year they were taken to Shifnal for a Confirmation service.

The Durant family pew in the Vernon Chantry.

A diary entry for 22nd January 1832 reads:

"Mr Robinson (the curate) preached a very good sermon. Fine. Maria rode round the wood and the kitchen garden, I walked by her. We saw Frank on the road by the Convent and heard he was sent back by the Bishop without getting priest's orders"

Frank was ordained deacon in 1831 after he graduating from Worcester College, Oxford. He had a curacy at Patshull, and was hoping to become Vicar of Tong, but the job went to his bastard brother. He asked his father for the ordination fees, but was refused. Durant thought the Bishop was right not to ordain him, because of his bad behaviour. Subsequently, he was priested, and held various chaplaincies in the area, but he never had a living.

There were also strange events. Once the pigs were poisoned. A servant, Mary Lee, was found drowned in the South Pool. Some thought a servant called Jenks had murdered her because she had his handkerchief in her hand. Using his authority as a J.P., Durant held a trial by ordeal to discover the culprit. However, on the appointed day, he sent Jenks (a favourite servant) to Lichfield, with two swans for his cousin, Archdeacon Buckeridge. No one was found guilty. Years later, on his deathbed, Jenks confessed to the murder. Mary Lee had gone to the pool to fill a kettle, and Jenks had pushed her in. At the end of his life, Jenks was in constant fear, and, if he saw a young woman coming towards him, he would rush into his house shouting, *"Shut the door. She is coming for me"*. Subsequently, a ghost appeared at the Castle. Some thought it was Mr Perry, who had accidentally shot himself many years before [10]. Others thought it was Mary Lee. Seven clergymen were summoned to lay the spirit, and they shut it up in a bottle. During the exorcism, 12 candles were lit, and five were suddenly blown out, four followed shortly after; only 3 were left. The bottle was secured, and deposited in the South Pool. In 1868, when the pool was drained for repairs, John Wedge found the bottle, and reburied it.

BEATI QUI DURANT is the family motto. The coat of arms, with the Fleur de Lys and the motto underneath, can still be seen on the iron posts around the entrance to the Castle, opposite the Old Post Office. The motto is a pun. It means either *"Blessed are they who endure"* or *"Blessed are the Durants"*. The arms seem to have been granted by the College of Heralds to another Durant family in 1634, but George commented on this: *"my arms were also there but no grant to them for as the family came from Normandy as gentlemen they wanted no grants in England"*. [11] We catch here, the possibility that the Durants invented a family history. One family paper claims that the family came over with William the Conqueror, like Roger de Montgomery. In 1833 George Stanton Eld, the son and heir, went on a search for their ancestral home, near Caen in Normandy. He thought it was the Chateau Virginie.

George (II)'s eccentricity and romanticisms reflects the Gothic fashion of the age. This is well expressed in his buildings. His father concentrated on the Castle, which was the first Gothic building in Shropshire, and the landscape. George (II)'s notebooks have drawings of the buildings that he erected around Tong. There is also a description of Convent Lodge as part of the ruins of the nunnery at Tong (which never existed). Many of the buildings had religious themes. The house called *"Cree Orchard"* became *"The Priory"* the cottage near the entrance to Ruckley was called *"Rosary Lodge"*. The female gatekeeper at Convent Lodge was dressed as a nun.

The Lectern Pulpit at Shrewsbury Abbey (old print)

Nearby was the so called *"Pulpit"*. This was a sort of gazebo, or summerhouse, put there so that George Durant could sit in it, and talk to his passing acquaintances. The design was a copy of the Refectory Lectern at Shrewsbury Abbey [12]. Much fiction became attached to this Pulpit. Some claimed it was used for preaching by Richard Baxter and John Wesley but both had died before it was built. Yet all these buildings could be a mockery of religion [13] in the manner of the Hell Fire Club and other contemporary customs of high society. [14]

Down the path from Convent Lodge, there was an archway made of Whalebones. Nearby was a cascade of water, and next to it an Hermitage. (See watercolour illustration in central section). It was occupied by a hermit, who known as *"Carolus"*. His real name was Charles Evans. He lived there for seven years, and died in 1822. A portrait of him by H. B. Hobday was exhibited at the Royal Academy. A retired soldier, called James Guidnet succeeded Evans, but he only stayed for a month. On the South Lawn of the Castle was a seat under a weeping willow made of iron, full of secret pipes. When anyone sat on an attached seat, the leaves poured water all over the unfortunate occupant. This was known as *"St Swithun's Chair"*

Durant put mottoes and inscriptions on his buildings. The Dove House (built in 1821, demolished in 1914) had over the door *"Pigeons only do know woe when a-beating they do go"*. On a gate to the Dingle were iron Aeolian harps on pillars, including these phrases from Thomas Moore's Irish Melodies:

"The harp that once through Tara's walls"
"No more to chiefs and ladies bright"

Nearby, on a spring, were the words:

"Adam's Ale Licensed to be drunk on the premises 1838."

The carpenter's shop, at Tong Norton, had a representation of a coffin on the wall with the words: *"In Morte Lucrum"* and *"Garde a vous"*.

The Egyptian Fowl House Pyramid next to Vauxhall Farm had many pictures of birds with inscriptions, including: *"Live and let live"*, *"Scratch before you peck"* and *"Teach your Granny"*.

The Blacksmith's Lodge at Ruckley Wood had tablets with the following inscription:

On the north side:
The hope in a future happier hour
That alights on misery's brow,
Springs like the silvery almond flower
That blooms on a leafless bough.
1843

On the cenotaph:
Strike with the iron hot
"Beati qui durant" and crest
O Stranger twine no wreath for me
But weave it of the cypress tree.
GD
HMVSP
Aet. 67

Auden comments that HMSVP were the surnames of the workmen who build the shop. The quotation was from Thomas Moore's **The Light of the Harem**, slightly altered. 67 was Durant's age; so these words were put up in the year before he died.

Durant's tenants had strict rules to follow (illustration page 64). The cottages had to be whitewashed, and the thatch kept in good repair. Chimneys were to be cleaned every two months, and the garden fence trimmed. Also churchgoing was an obligation. They had to promise

"I moreover engage that at least one Person in my Family shall attend Divine service every Sabbath-day or in default thereof that I will forfeit six pence for each and every neglect."

In his attitudes and interests Durant was typical of his age. Much of this was an expression of the new appetite for Gothic imitation. Both Pains Hill, in Surrey, and Hawkstone Hall, near Hodnet, had a hermit well before Tong.

In 1837, Durant held a remarkable Aquatic Tournament, (illustration page 65) probably to raise money for the restoration of Tong Church. It was an imitation of an event, which Lord Eglington had organised a month before. **The Shrewsbury Chronicle** described the event:

"At an early hour in Monday morning the village of Tong was rendered very sprightly and gay by the arrival of visitors from all parts to witness the Tournament: a spectacle likely to become popular. Upon the pound near the lake, refreshment booths were erected and kept by Col Durant's tenants, who exerted themselves to make the public honour them with their merry company. At ten o'clock the whole space about the water was surrounded by coaches, omnibuses, carriages, chaises, gigs etc... which still continued to pour in from all directions; in fact the tout ensemble at this time was gay and brilliant in the extreme. The fresh breeze from the water tempering the heat and the crowds of handsome female spectators splendidly attired gave the whole scene an air of enchanting, yet refined hilarity. Shortly after this hour it began to rain in torrents. By 12 the rain ceased. The sound of martial music was heard proceeding from the castle, and the minstrels were seen making for the lake with the 12 champions in front. Shortly afterwards Col Durant's carriage drawn by four beautiful horses, richly caparisoned emerged from the castle and proceeded towards the lake, where it was received with cheers and shouts that were heard for miles. When the carriage with Miss C Durant, Queen of Beauty, and other ladies emerged, the music played "Conquering hero". They embarked for the Fairy isle. Musicians were on another island. Each boat when tilting contained two rowers, a champion and a trumpeter for attack signals. It continued until about 4 o'clock, when the

victor Abraham Hounslow, was rowed in triumph to the fairy isle where he received a purse of gold from the fair hand of the young Queen. She wore a satin dress beautifully ornamented with gold and a handsome crown of pearls interwoven with flowers." [15]

What are we to make of this strange man? Here was a rich landowner, a member of a clerical family; an affectionate father to his children when young; a Colonel in the Shropshire Militia and a Justice of the Peace. However, this was a man with few friends. He involved himself in litigation; built eccentric buildings; could not leave women alone, and was hated by his children. His descendant Dr St George of New Zealand has suggested that he might have been a schizophrenic. Whatever the causes, Tong would be a very different place without the Durants.

George Durant (II) died on the 18th November 1844. The Shrewsbury Chronicle recorded the event as follows:

"George Durant died from ossification of the heart, a disease from which he had long suffered. When he felt that he could not much longer survive he sent for a master carpenter from Shifnal and gave him instructions to prepare his coffin from a plan which he had committed to writing. When the coffin was finished it was brought to Tong Castle and by the dying man's instructions taken up to his room. On seeing it he wept for some time but on becoming calm expressed his approval of the work. The coffin was made of Spanish mahogany. It was seven foot long, two feet six inches wide and three inches thick. The shape of it was that of a sarcophagus and within it were a complete shell and lead coffin. On the outside was carved the Arms of the Durant family... This was likewise repeated on the massive mahogany bands which encircled the sides. At the foot of the lid was a raised cross and twenty carved rosettes framed an effective border. The inscription on the lid as follows 'Beati Qui Durant / George Durant Esq. Of Tong Castle / Born April 25th 1776 / Died November 29th 1844 / Spes Mea Christus.'" [16]

That night, the villagers of Tong did not sleep well. As soon as he heard the news, Ernest Durant mounted his horse, and galloped through the village shouting, *"The old man's dead at last"*. At the suggestion of their late brother George, Ernest and Frank gathered together a number of workmen from the estate. They went up to the offensive monument on the Knoll that their father had erected to his corrupt solicitor. They placed 70 lbs of gunpowder underneath, and blew it up. The explosion shook the Village. Some thought the end of the world had come. The stone, with the offensive inscription, was ground into powder and mixed into a heap of manure. Justice was done at last! George Durant was buried in the family vault underneath the Chancel of the Church.

The Will of George Durant (II) was the subject of considerable litigation. The Will was drafted in 1837, and was subject to various codicils, as his family fell out of favour. Arthur Edwin was to be left one shilling, and no more because of *"improper conduct"*. Frank was left 10 shillings, but had to pay back £100 to the Executors. Edwin Orlando gets 10 shillings *"Because he is well off"*. He refers to the *"unnatural and undutiful conduct"* of his sons. The servants get half a year's wages, and all labourers an extra month's pay. There was also a considerable legal wrangle over the Ruckley Estate, which Durant had purchased in 1772.

Celeste moved from the Castle to Tong Hall, and then to London. She also inherited Childwick Hall, but it was later sold. She lived in Brussels with her children for some time. In 1860, she returned to London. She had three different residences, before dying at 10, Southbank Terrace, Kensington, in 1876. She was buried in the Roman Catholic Cemetery at Mortlake. The heir to the estate was George (II)'s grandson George Chares Selwyn Durant. He was 16 years old.

The Durant legacy cannot be ignored. It embodies many aspects of human experience; good and evil; suffering and exploitation; romance and fantasy; power and frailty, and the effect people have on each other and the environment. There is a sense in which the motto, BEATI QUI DURANT, has been prophetic. The way the Durants treated the whole village as a private domain, over which they presided, conditioned the social atmosphere. The Durant aura has persisted. It has given Tong a remarkable story and has helped to preserve the identity of the village.

NOTES

[1] *The Shrewsbury Chronicle* November 1844. There is a fine portrait of Mr Eld of Seighford by Joshua Reynolds which is now in the Museum of Art in Boston, Mass. It used to belong to Stoke on Trent Hospital.

[2] Quoted by Bath.

[3] These proceedings are described in the history of the St George family but are part of the court case in *English Reports Vol 162 on Durant v Durant*. In the family papers the account has been cut out.

[4] I have a photograph of this typical monument in the cemetery with a Maltese cross on the top; sent to me by a correspondent in Paris, but on visits have been unable to locate it.

[5] Childwick had been an estate of 900 acres and had been developed by Joshua Lomax in 1674. It was described as *"a substantial seat, the original restrained elegance of which is still attested to by the old stable block"*. Lomax left the estate to his son. It is not clear from whom Durant purchased it. See L. Stone *An Open Elite* pp117ff.

[6] Quoted in Auden Vol 1

[7] Papers recently found in the Lichfield Diocesan Archives. They are not in the family papers. Defamation of Character was an Ecclesiastical Offence until 1855.

[8] For Chrysom's cemetery see Chapter 7.

[9] The reference is to Edwin Durant who had come home from India and married his cousin Elizabeth Buckeridge. They were returning to India.

[10] Mr Perry was a friend of Mr Plowden who rented the Castle before George Durant (II) came of age He came in through a window with a loaded shotgun, which went off. There were bloodstains on the floor ever after. His tombstone is in the churchyard.

[11] Quoted by Bath

[12] This still can be seen in a garden opposite the Abbey. The one at Tong collapsed in the 1970s.

[13] This suggestion is made by Headley and Meulenkamp in their book *Follies*. See Epilogue.

[14] See V. Murray *High Society in the Regency Period 1788-1830*.

[15] *The Shrewsbury Chronicle*

[16] See [1] above

The colour illustrations on the centre pages of this book show a portrait of George Durant (1st) painted by Sir Joshua Reynolds in 1761 between his two West Indian expeditions. They also include a series of watercolours from George Durant II's notebook of assorted buildings that he erected at Tong reproduced by kind permission of Lady Higgs.

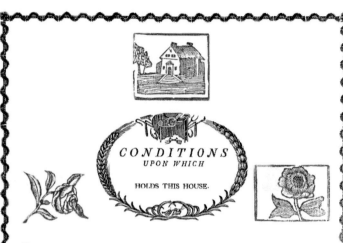

CONDITIONS
UPON WHICH

HOLDS THIS HOUSE.

I do hereby promife to keep this Houfe, which I hold under *G. Durant Efq.* of *Tong Caftle* in the County of *Salop*, in good and creditable Repair. That it fhall be always well Thatched, Glazed, and White-wafhed. The Garden Fence neatly trimmed; the Chimney fwept once in two Months; and the Rent, being *L.* paid Half-Yearly, on 25*th* March, and 29*th* September. I moreover engage, that at least one Perfon in my Family, fhall attend Divine Service every Sabbath-day, or in default thereof, that I will forfeit Sixpence for each and every neglect; to be paid immediately to the Clerk of the Parifh, one third for himfelf, the rest to be distributed amongst the Alms-houfe Widows. And at any time, on receiving Six Months Notice, will peaceably deliver up this Houfe and Pre-mifes to *G. Durant, Efq.* or his Reprefentative.

Approved. Signed.
G. DURANT.

Witneffed
Tong Castle, September 1, 1804.

Tenants Agreement 1804

Aquatic Tournament,

ON THE LAKE AT TONG,

September 16th, 1839, at Twelve o'Clock.

AS EXHIBITED IN FRANCE AND BELGIUM.

A PURSE OF GOLD

WILL BE AWARDED TO THE VICTOR;

AND ONE OF SILVER

To the SECOND CHAMPION; with a handsome Gratuity to the unsuccessful Competitors, and the Families of those who fall *Hors de Combat*, by the QUEEN of LOVE and BEAUTY (elected for the occasion) from the Fairy Isle.

TO CONCLUDE WITH

A Coracle Race for the Ladies' Purse.

☞ The Band will be stationed on the Western Island, and the commencement announced by the Discharge of Cannon.

☞ Tickets of Admission will be given on Application to Mr. LEES, of the Bell Inn; Mrs. DOWNING, of the Bush Tavern; and Mr. BOTHAM, of Tong;—by whom Refreshments will be provided in the Tents in the Wood by the Lake Side.

W. PARKE, PRINTER, WOLVERHAMPTON.

Notice of the Aquatic Tournament 1837

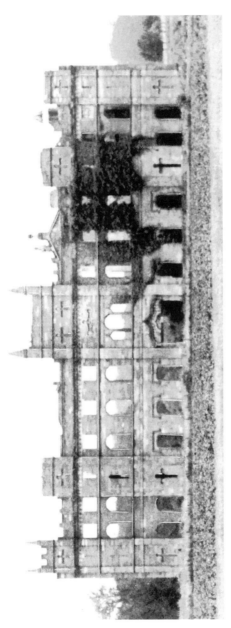

Tong Castle 1954
(photograph by permission of the Shropshire Star)

Chapter 5
The Decline and Fall of Tong Castle

By the time that George Durant (II) had died, his son and heir was already dead. George Stanton Eld Durant never got on with his father. He went on the Grand Tour when he was twenty and tried to find the so-called original Durant ancestral home in Normandy. Around the same time, he met Lucinda Saunders and they were married at the British Embassy chapel in Paris without his father's knowledge or approval. They lived in Brussels for sometime, where they had two children. Later, they moved to London, where a second daughter was born. His father had kept him very short of money and Mr Bishton of Kilsall had helped him out financially. Following his marriage, to help with his finances George (III) mortgaged his expected inheritance. This greatly displeased his father, who was himself thus unable to raise money for himself. George and Lucinda lived in London and Sussex and he died in Harley Street, London at the age of thirty in 1831. He is buried in the Churchyard at Tong with his brother Frank. Both were denied the family vault.

After the death of George (II), his grandson George Charles Selwyn (IV) moved into the Castle with his mother and two sisters. He had been alienated from his grandfather, and on arrival, made changes at the Castle. The servants were given new liveries; the dressmakers were moved from the Dovecote. Two houses and the laundry, where his grandfather's nefarious affairs had taken place, were pulled down. His mother hated Tong, and they only lived there in the winter. The houses in London and Childwick Hall were rented out.

He went to Magdalen College Oxford in 1847, but did not take a degree. Instead, he purchased a commission in the 12th Lancers. When he came of age in April 1849, a party was held at the Castle. During the party the Tong Park Farm buildings were burned down. Between 1851 and 1854 he served in the Cape, the East Indies and at the Crimean War. He became a Captain in 1853. During most of this time, a caretaker called Langford looked after the Castle. The third 30-year lease came to and end in 1854, and Lucinda persuaded her son to sell the Castle. It had not been well maintained. Part of the cellars had to be filled in to support the structure.

The Castle and the Estate were sold by Auction on Tuesday 11th September 1855. It was sold in two lots. Everything, except the Ruckley

Wood Estate and Farm, was sold to the Earl of Bradford for £171,500. The Ruckley Estate went to John Jones for £6,700. The paintings were not included in the sale. The Tong Estate sale was conditional on the purchaser maintaining the chancel of Tong Church (hence the restoration of the church in 1892). He also had to pay £34p.a. for the maintenance of the Almshouses. The population was 500, and very few were described as poor. George Durant left the Army in 1856, and married in 1871. He died, in Ealing, seven months later, having fallen from a window of the Star and Garter Hotel in Richmond. Some suspected that it was suicide. His mother, Lucinda, died on March 15th 1876.

Lord Bradford let the Castle to Mr John Hartley, and his brother-in-law Thomas Thorneycroft. Hartley was born in Dumbarton in 1813. A Methodist and a very religious man he was connected with Wesleyan Methodism in Wolverhampton and Birmingham.

He was a glass manufacturer in the firm of Chance & sons. He married Emma the second daughter of George Thorneycroft in 1839. He had three

John Hartley Esq

daughters and one son who became a Methodist minister. He then became an ironmaster in the firm Thorneycroft, Hartley, Kesteven & Perks. He was mayor of Wolverhampton in 1858. Later he was Deputy Lieutenant of Staffordshire and High Sheriff in 1870. He died in 1884, but his widow continued the tenancy until her death in 1909. The Hartleys are buried in Tong Churchyard. They seem to have been very hospitable people, who entertained on a grand scale. We have already seen how Mr Durant's Aquatic Tournament brought in the crowds, and now Tong became a popular place for outings from the West Midlands. We catch a glimpse of this in one of the novels of E. T. Fowler. She was John Hartley's niece, and in **The Farringdons** (1901) she described a Whit Monday outing to Tong Castle (She calls Tong "Pembruge"):

"At last they came to a picturesque wall and gateway built of the red stone which belongs to that part of the country, and which has a trick of growing so much redder at evening time that it looks as if the cold stone were blushing with pleasure at being kissed

good night by the sun: and then through a wood sloping on the left down to a little stream, which was so busy talking to itself about its own concerns that it had no time to leap and sparkle for the amusement of passers-by; until they drew up in front of a quaint old castle built of the same stone as the outer walls and gateway.

The family were away from home, so the whole castle was at the disposal of Alan and his party, and they had permission to go wherever they liked. The state-rooms were in front of the building and led out of each other so that when all the doors were open anyone could see right from one end of the castle to the other. Dinner was to be served in the large saloon at the back, built over what was once the courtyard; and while the servants were laying the tables with cold viands, which they had brought with them. Alan took his guests through the staterooms to see the pictures, and endeavoured to carry out his plan of educating them by pointing out to them some of the finer works of art.

'This' he said stopping in front of a portrait, 'is a picture of Lady Mary Wortley Montague who was born here, painted by one of the finest portrait painters of her day.'"[1]

(Not only does this reveal Hartley's hospitality, but also we see her continuing the false stories about Tong. Lady Mary Wortley Montagu was not born there, and she was already married when her uncle inherited the Castle. Moreover the finest paintings were removed before the 1854 auction).

The Hartleys played a major role in the life of the Church, and the community. Miss Auden, a daughter of the Revd. J .E Auden, told me that, as a child, she used to play with the Hartley children. Mrs Christabel Werstley (Mrs Hartley's great grand-daughter) recalled splendid Christmas celebrations. However, all the events took place on the ground floor, because the upper rooms were not safe. At the slightest shower of rain, hipbaths had to be placed all over the building to catch the water, which was pouring through the roof. [2]

When Mrs Hartley died in 1909, it was decided to sell the remaining contents of the Castle. The sale catalogue listed the contents. [3] There were nearly 1,000 items, plus the contents of 25 Bedrooms, and 18 reception rooms. There were still 130 oil paintings, and six carriages. There were 759 books; 161 bottles of wine; musical instruments; crockery; cutlery, and vast amounts of furniture. The sale took place over 3 days at the end of September. Mr Ingram Brown told me that he attended with his father, taking their purchases away in a horse and cart. [4] During the sale, the main staircase fell in.

Lord Bradford tried again to find a purchaser for the building, but failed. So in 1916, the lead was stripped off the roof, and various fixtures like fireplaces were removed. Some items were shipped to America. During this demolition, a large picture called *"The Garden of Eden"* was found rolled up in a ceiling. [5] It sold for £3,000.

The decay of the Castle continued. Loads of brick and stone were removed to fill in hollows, and make up farm roads on the estate. People still came out from Wolverhampton to picnic in the grounds. During the Second World War, a large number of huts were erected in the grounds to house families from RAF Cosford.

After a child, from Tong Park Farm, was killed playing in the ruins, it was clear that the structure was dangerous. It was decided to demolish the Castle. On the night before the demolition, two girls from the village reported that they had encountered the ghost of a monk leaving the Castle. [6] Then, on 18th July 1954, a large crowd gathered to watch this historic event (illustration page 71). The operation was conducted by the 213 Field Squadron Royal Engineers (T.A.). 208 boreholes were placed around the building, using 136 lbs of plastic explosive, and 75lbs of amatol. The Church windows were opened to cope with the blast. At 2.30 p.m. Lord Newport fired the charges. There are some fine photographs of this event, with the whole base of the Castle covered in smoke. A great cloud of dust and debris covered most of the buildings in the village. Tong Castle was no more.

Among the people attending was Anthony Durant (later the M.P. for Reading). [7] It was an event that the first and second George Durants could not have imagined.

In the 1960s the New Town of Telford was developed out of the old towns around Ironbridge, and it was essential that there was a main trunk road, linking Telford with the West Midlands. Once the route was established, going through the site of the Castle, local pressure demanded that an archaeological rescue was required. This was contrary to the wishes of the Local Authority. Mr Alan Wharton established the Tong Archaeological Group, using Convent Lodge as a base and conducted the work between 1974 and 1980. Mr Durant's Ice House was removed to the Avoncroft Museum of Buildings. Major discoveries were made. [8]

The Destruction of Tong Castle 1954
(photograph by permission of the Shropshire Star)

Thus the main feudal home in the area had become Weston Park, which has continued to play a role in the area. It hosted a meeting of the G8 with President Clinton; mock Civil War battles; pop concerts; and occasional ecclesiastical meetings, in the process of appointing a new Bishop of Lichfield. In Tong only the Church is left, standing for the past history of the Village. The story of the College and the Church must now be told.

NOTES

[1] E. T. Fowler *The Farringdons* p102. See also Chapter 13.
[2] Article in *The Shropshire Magazine* 1984
[3] *Tong Castle Catalogue of the Sale of the Contents* T. J. Barnett & Sons. Wolverhampton. 1909
[4] Ingram Brown's father farmed near Sherriffhales. This was before he took on Tong Park Farm.
[5] The 1786 catalogue says this was in the Principal Dining Room and is entitled "Adam and Eve naming the Creation", being 11ft 6 by 9ft 6.
[6] According to Mrs Margaret Brown.
[7] *Wolverhampton Express & Star* July 19th 1954
[8] See Reports of the Tong Archaeological Group

View of the Durant Castle from the garden

Part Two: Ecclesiastical Tong

Chapter 6

Tong College

Roger de Montgomery's Church had been served by monks from Shrewsbury Abbey. The early fifteenth century saw a change in the arrangements with the establishment of Tong College. We have seen the machinations of the Vernons over Shottesbrooke, but, from this, came the model for Tong College. Sir Fulke and Isabel Pembrugge began to plan Tong College before 1405. [1] Property had to be purchased to generate income for the College. Shottesbrooke gave them some idea of the costs involved. It also provided a model for the College statures. So we read of property deals, and the appointment of clergy. The setting up of a Collegiate Church was a complex matter, which required costly Papal, Episcopal and Royal Licenses. [2] Isabel purchased the advowson (to appoint the clergy) from the Abbot of Shrewsbury for £40.

Fulke died in 1409, and Isabel established the Church and College so that masses might be said for her three husbands. The founding of Collegiate Churches was fashionable at this time. One reason for this was the Black Death. [3] The Bubonic Plague had arrived in England in 1348 and recurred in 1361, 1362, and 1369. It continued sporadically, until the end of the seventeenth century. It affected the whole of society. Sixty percent of Europe's population died in the process. Armies were depleted, and labour became scarce. By 1400, landowners had difficulty to find enough tenants to care for the land. As a result, the labourers gained some power. A class of richer peasants emerged, who were able to make demands on the landowners. This was a factor in the Peasant's Revolt of 1381. Another result of the Black Death was the development of the English language. After the Norman Conquest, French was the language of the ruling classes but many French teachers died and others returned to France. Also the Hundred Years War developed a strong anti-French feeling and the English language began to come into its own.

The massive increase in sudden deaths led to a great desire to pray for the dead. The Battle of Shrewsbury in 1403 led to the establishment of Battlefield College, with 8 clergy to pray for the souls of those, who died in that massive slaughter. There were different sorts of Colleges. Some provided singers for cathedrals; some were attached to hospitals; some included academic institutions; and others (like Tong) were Chantries. Part of this was a reaction against Monasteries. They had developed vast wealth, and people became suspicious of their increasing power. So the rich became more inclined to endow their own Colleges and Chantries, to pray for the dead and to provide some local education. Thus, by 1540, there were over 2,000 Chantries and colleges. The poor could never afford a building, but Guilds paid for masses to be said. The very poor would simple light a candle.

There is no knowledge of the state of the earlier Church at Tong, but there was a chapel in the Castle. This is indicated by the discovery of an early 14th century pewter cruet (for communion wine) during the Castle excavation. [4]

The College was built on the south side of the Church and had various ancillary buildings. These included a hospice for 13 elderly and infirm people. The Royal Licence of Henry IV, establishing the College, was granted in 1410. It granted approval, to Walter Swan, Clerk, and William Mosse, Clerk, to acquire the Church, the patronage, and to build the new Church and College. Swan was the incumbent of Pembridge in Herefordshire. The College was to have five chaplains and a Warden. The first Warden was installed in 1411. The College was to celebrate daily Divine services:

"for your prosperity while we are alive and that of Thomas Beaufort, our brother and the afore said Isabel while they are alive and moreover for our souls when we have migrated from this life, and those of our ancestors and that of aforesaid Fulke; and moreover for souls of Margaret his wife and of Thomas Peytevene, knight, and of John Ludlow, knight and also the souls of the parents and all the ancestors of the aforesaid Isabel and all the faithful departed, according to the regulation of the aforesaid Isabel, Walter and William their heirs or assignees, to be made for this purpose."

The deed gave the details of how the College was to be financed. The patronage was arranged so that after Isabel's death, it was to be transferred to her heirs, through Richard Vernon. The statutes followed those of Shottesbrooke College, which had been established in 1337. The Revd J. E. Auden has given an overall picture of College life. [5] Each of the five members of the College had their own duties:

"The Warden had the general supervision of the whole establishment. One priest was sub Warden, another Steward; a fourth was parochial chaplain, a fifth Schoolmaster. Their lives were by no means idle. Every day, winter and summer, they were called by the Church bell to their places in Choir…. Here they would say Matins and Prime together, and the corresponding Hours of the Blessed Virgin Mary. Then immediately would follow her mass in her special Chapel on the north side of the Church. At this mass, all the chaplains' clerks and paupers were bound to be present, unless certain of the first happened to be officiating at Masses for the founders and benefactors at other altars. Then would come the High Mass of the day. This finished there might be a meeting of the College chapter. Following this, probably Pittance, a simple meal of bread and water, though no mention of this is mentioned in the statutes. Then at 9 a.m. Terce would be said in church. Afterwards would come the secular work of the day and each chaplain departs to his own special duty; the Warden to his cell to arrange the multitudinous affairs of the college, the sub-warden to the oversight of the details of the church services and to the care of the library; the Steward to his accounts of the incomings and outgoings of the college or the storage or giving out of provisions required for the whole establishment; the parochial chaplain to visit the sick among the parishioners in the village; the Schoolmaster to teach the choristers and the children of the neighbourhood. After Sext at noon, the mid-day meal in the refectory which was eaten in silence while one of the clerks or a chorister read passages from some holy book. Then back to their work again, interrupted at 3 p.m. by None in the Church: these said secular duties again till the evening meal. Then soon would ring the bell for vespers and Compline and the office of the dead. And all this over, they would retire to rest in their dormitory. The life of the chaplains at Tong would be one of rigorous discipline under Rule… But it was not a hard life, and the enjoyment of a month's holiday each year was the right of everyone." [6]

The clergy were celibate, but they were not monks, and could possess property. Three of the five were not allowed to hold any other appointment. There were two other clerks (in lower orders), who were really College servants. Their role was to wait on the members of the College, and to sing in the choir, assisted by some local boys. On election the Warden had to be presented to the Bishop of Coventry and Lichfield. [7] Later, Wardens were to be elected by the College from its members, and the name submitted to the patron. If the College could not agree, the patron would appoint. The Warden had to keep the accounts and the Inventory; administer discipline; supervise the servants and paupers; and hear everyone's Confession once a year. If the Warden was away, the Sub Warden was in charge.

Payment was made for work done. The Parochial Chaplain and the Schoolmaster received additional payments. Those, who failed to attend services, were fined halfpence a time. The College building must have been quite big; meals were eaten in a common refectory. All talk had to be in a subdued tone. The door was locked at night, and the Warden kept the key. A Steward or Cellarer was appointed to deal with provisions. [8] There are rules for entertaining visitors:

"The brothers are to abstain, as far as they can, from the introduction of strangers that the ground of distraction may be cut away as much as can be done honourably."

No one was to invite women into the College, however respectable, except on rare occasions and for approved reasons. But no woman of doubtful character could be admitted. If someone was entertained, the person inviting was responsible for the payment of the meal. (Three pence at the high table, and half that at the lower table). Leisure activities were allowed, but strictly controlled:

"no priest or clerk of the said College is to indulge in noisy hunting, or in any other kind of hunting or hawking especially at the time in which he is bound to be present there at matins, mass and the other canonical hours or the rest of the appointed and accustomed Offices: nor to keep within the enclosure any hunting dog specially owned by him, though it be of very beautiful colour, unless licence has been unanimously granted him by the consent of the Warden or others, or the burden of the said house."

Crimes and faults are to be confessed to the brethren and penance performed. An offending brother may be re-admitted to the fellowship but adultery, incest, perjury, false witness, sacrilege, theft and robbery, if committed more than once, could be a reason for expulsion. Lesser crimes did not carry this penalty, unless there was no restoration after three warnings. These are listed as simple fornication; disobedience; rebellion, brawling; constant gluttony; or drunkenness. Members of the College could leave, if they gave six month's notice. This enabled a successor to be found.

There may have been two other centres of worship as well as the Church. One was in the hospice; the other was a chapel in the Castle. In the Church, the pattern of worship followed the Sarum rite. As at Shottesbrooke, we find this expressed by the Easter sepulchre in the Sanctuary. (This was used to keep a watch before Easter Day). High Mass each day had a special intention.

Sunday	Mass of the Holy Trinity
Monday	Mass of the Holy Ghost
Tuesday	Mass for the Salvation of Men
Wednesday	Mass of the Angels
Thursday	Mass of the Corpus Christi
Friday	Mass of the Holy Cross
Saturday	Requiem Mass

Major festivals would take precedence over the intentions. If paupers were too ill Mass would be said for them in the hospice chapel. Requiem masses were also said on the following dates:

27th May	For Fulke de Pembrugge and his wife
20th July	For Sir John Ludlow
15th November	For Sir Thomas Peytevene
30th November	For Sir Ralph Lingen

And for Isabel, William Mosse and Walter Swann on the anniversaries of their deaths.

These masses and others would have increased the College income.

In 1510, Sir Henry Vernon added his own Chantry chapel. He used income, from land in Walsall and West Bromwich, to pay for an extra priest. This Chantry priest lived in the College. Henry strengthened the college by his endowments and the Chantry chaplain appointed was John Coley. He was to be a member of the College and to take up his position *"without any presentation, admission, institution or induction."*

There were 13 Wardens during the lifetime of the College. One of them, Richard Eyton, was Warden for 42 years (1437-79).

The College influenced the economic life of the parish. The financial basis of the College lay in the possession of income-producing land. It was not all local; there were lands in Northamptonshire, Leicestershire and Cambridgeshire. In 1415 the Manor and Grange of Lapley was added togther with *"All lands tenements, rents, services, leases, annuities, shares, pensions, mills, meadows, pastures, waters, ways, footpaths, fishponds, together with the feudal services of soldiers and advowsons of Churches and other ecclesiastical benefices".*

The Warden kept fishponds at Wheaton Aston. The College also acquired Weston-under-Lizard, and some lands at Wellington (Shropshire). The members of the College were fed, and paid six marks a year. The revised statutes raised the stipends. The hospice was vested in the Lord of the Manor, and had its own Warden. A local Guild of All Saints received

£20 p.a. and the paupers were to be given two shillings a week, plus adequate supplies of corn and meat. The revised statutes of 1423 increased the payments to the Warden and the Chaplains, but later accounts reveal that they were not always paid.

The accounts for 1437 and 1440 reveal that the College was employing five farm servants. By this time, it was providing enough corn, meat, and dairy products to meet all the requirements of the community. In 1438, the College was able to sell surplus rye and wool. In 1432, they had 92 sheep and 30 stones of wool were sold. By 1441, the amount of wool went up to 39 stones. There was a vineyard situated to the south east of the College.

A group of five or six clergy at Tong would not have been unusual at this time. In 1500, the population of England was 2 million, and there were 23,500 clergy. Every resident in Tong would have been, in some way, connected to the Castle and the College. So here was a compact, and self-sufficient community. The closure of the College must have been a threat to communal life, through the ending of education and a reduction in employment.

As part of the dissolution of the monasteries and religious houses, Henry VIII authorised a survey of all ecclesiastical revenues. The value of the Church, annexed to the College was £6.13.4d, less 14s due to the Bishop. The College endowments were £45.9s.10d, with £22.8s.1d annual income. £6s. 8d was due to the Abbot of Shrewsbury for the advowson.

Tong was one of the last Colleges to be dissolved in the lifetime of King Henry VIII. It took place on 27th and 29th September 1546. The owner of Tong was George Vernon. We note, with interest, the names of the four commissioners to seize the College. They were George Vernon, Thomas Giffard, Francis Cave and George Blount. They were all people with local knowledge. George Blount was Lord of the Manor of Kinlet, and had seized Battlefield College. Giffard owned nearby Chillington. He acquired White Ladies Priory in 1535, and Blackladies in 1539. The College of Tong and the Vernon Chantry were granted by King Edward VI to Sir Richard Manners. He was the 4th son of the Earl of Ros, and brother of the first Earl of Rutland. He was also the third husband of Margaret Dymoke (who had been married to Richard Vernon) and was probably living at Tong at the time. The permission to receive the College was given by the Recorder of London. [9] Richard purchased Lapley and all the Tong possessions for £486 in 1547. Then he sold Lapley to Robert Broke for £476, and the Tong lands to James Woolriche for £200, thus making a tidy profit. (Woolriche was one of only two private landowners in Tong). The College lands and the buildings remained in the Woolriche family until purchased by William Pierrepoint. This reintegrated the Tong lands.

The College was fought over during the Civil War. In April 1644, Col. Tiller, in a letter to Prince Rupert, states that he had driven the rebels out of the Church, and then out of the College and the Castle. He considered the Castle was worth keeping, but suggested that the College should be demolished. In the excavations of the College there was a level that indicated that it had been burned down around this time. [10] The hospice remained occupied until George Durant replaced it with the almshouses, which were built early in the nineteenth century. In 1757, the hospice had a thatched roof. [11] There is no record of the clergy at Tong until 1602. The Duke of Kingston provided a new Vicarage on the old College land in 1725.

The Church with its choir stalls, screens and Chantry stands as a reminder of its Collegiate foundation.

NOTES

[1] Papers at Belvoir Castle.
[2] P. Jeffery *The Collegiate Churches of England and Wales*. For Battlefield see also the paper by P. Morgan (see Bibliography). It may be significant that Battlefield was refounded in 1410.
[3] See P. Ziegler *The Black Death* and O. J Benedictow *The Black Death*
[4] A. Wharton *Tong Archaeological Group Report*
[5] Paper on Tong College in the transactions of Shropshire Archaeological Society.
[6] Ibid
[7] In 1410 this was John Burghill, a Dominican who was confessor to King Richard II. He died in 1414.
[8] A memorial brass to Ralph Elcock the cellarer is on the south wall of the Church.
[9] This document and the papers concerning the founding of the College are in the archives at Belvoir Castle.
[10] A. Wharton
[11] Reported by Cole in *The Gentleman's Magazine*

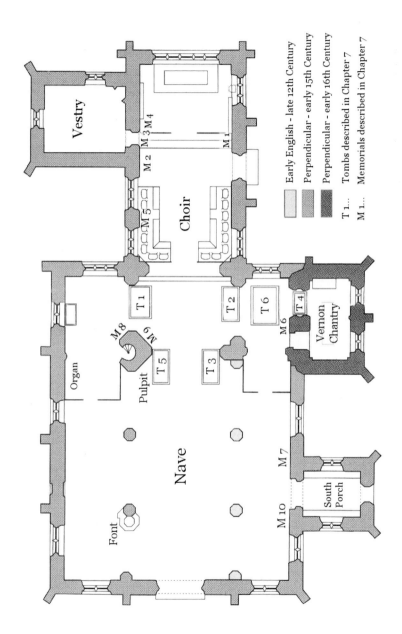

Vestry

Choir

M 2 M 5 M 3 M 4 M 1

T 1

T 2

T 6

T 4

M 6

Vernon Chantry

M 8 M 9

T 5

T 3

Pulpit

Organ

Nave

Font

M 7

M 10

South Porch

Early English - late 12th Century

Perpendicular - early 15th Century

Perpendicular - early 16th Century

T 1... Tombs described in Chapter 7

M 1... Memorials described in Chapter 7

Plan of Tong Church

Chapter 7
Tong Church

The Churches and Churchyards of England are a vital source of local history. In them, we find the influences, which have shaped and created community. In an elusive way, we see how Christian insights, values, worship, preaching and teaching have acted as a leaven in the lump of society.

The first Church was built by Roger de Montgomery (along with one at Donnington) in 1087, but it is not easy to date the present Church. It was being planned as early as 1406. What is very striking is the way its architecture is derived from that of Shottesbrooke Church, which was built in 1337. It also has three entrances, and a central tower, and built all on one level (as Tong was until the restoration of 1892.) Whereas Shottesbrooke is built mainly in the local Berkshire flint, Tong is built in the local red sandstone. Both are integrated buildings, built at one period, and both are lightly restored. [1]

There are many descriptions of Tong Church. The earlier ones help us to see what happened at the Victorian restoration. Archdeacon Cranage wrote his description, just after its restoration. He describes it as *"a most interesting building"* of *"perpendicular character"*, and admires the restoration work. There is an octagonal central Tower, and within it rises the central spire altered by Sir Henry Vernon, so that it could contain the Great Bell of Tong. Above it, are six bells, and a Sanctus Bell. The bells are rung from the middle of the church. Ringing is not easy, because the floor slopes from the east to the west end. The slope may be due to the bedrock, but some have thought it was constructed to enable the Church to be cleaned easily. Water poured out at the East end would automatically run to the West.

The exterior of the building gives the impression of having a low elevation. This is because the low roofs are concealed beneath battlemented parapets. Pinnacles appear at regular intervals along the roof. There are some fine gargoyles. Pevsner says that the interior is not easy to take in, because of the tombs and monuments, [2] whereas Petrie comments that the architecture gives the effect of scale and proportion. [3] Low old pews surround the visitor, many dating back to the sixteenth century. Many of them were altered at the Victorian restoration. The original three screens, at the end of the nave and the aisles, are still in place. They date from the fifteenth century.

Interior of Tong Church pre-restoration

Interior of Shottesbrooke Church

The font is at the west end. The wooden pulpit, by the northwest pier of the Tower is Jacobean. In the north Aisle is the former Lady Chapel. A small organ was installed in 1877. The Chancel, where the members of the College sat for the daily offices, contains sixteen choir stalls with misericords. The return stall seat, for the College Warden, has an

Annunciation scene with a lily in the centre with a crucifix emerging from it. This design reflects a long tradition that Jesus' crucifixion took place on the anniversary of the Annunciation. This demonstrates that Mary and Jesus share a common suffering. There are very few depictions left since the Reformation and Tong is unique in being on a misericord. [4] The end of the stall has a fine carving of the Ascension.

Drawing of the Lily Crucifix miserecord

The fifth stall on the south side is of special interest. This is the only stall, with carving rather than decoration, at the top. On the right hand side is an angel, holding a shield on which are signs of the passion. This represents a typical form of devotion of the time. On the left is a face, (possibly a "Veronica") which is very like the one on the Turin Shroud. Beneath both is an heraldic bird. The bird is that of the de Weston crest, which can be seen in the neighbouring Church at Weston-under-Lizard. In that Church are two tombs of de Westons. They were crusaders, and members of the Knights Templar. At one time, the Knights Templar claimed to posses the Turin Shroud, and they had a devotion to the face of

Christ. On the seat below is the carving of a Green Man. So the whole stall becomes a meditation on faces.

The door to the vestry has three large holes in it. There has been much speculation about the purpose of these holes. It could have been to enable the servers to see what was happening at the High Altar during the liturgy. The vestry is small and square and part of the original building. The large oak cupboards on the west wall were put in to house the Tong Minster's Library (see Chapter 8). A fireplace and chimney were added to preserve the books.

In the sanctuary, there are two niches each side of the altar, which once contained statues of St Bartholomew and Our Lady. They were destroyed, either at the Reformation, or during the Civil War. The wooden reredos, installed as part of the 1898 restoration, has figures on it, which were carved at Oberammergau. The east window was designed by Charles Kempe. He rescued all the 15th century glass he could find, and put it in the west window. It depicts Edmund King and Martyr, an angel holding a shield and a few other pieces. Earlier the window had been smaller. The new window is similar to that east window in Haddon Hall Chapel (the other seat of the Vernons). On the south side of the sanctuary, is a less interesting window, commemorating the restoration work funded by Lord Bradford.

We see another effect of the Civil War in the cannon ball marks on the outside of the north aisle and a remaining stone cannon ball is in the Vestry.

TOMBS

1) The tombs trace the history of Tong and begin with the founders of the Church and College. Sir Fulke and Dame Isabel de Pembrugge lie on the north side of the tower. The images are made of Nottingham alabaster, as are two others. [5] Sir Fulke's head rests on a helmet, depicting a Turkish slave with plaited hair. Fulke is dressed in chain mail. Isabel is dressed as a widow and black paint can still be seen in the folds of he dress. At her feet is a fawn, which has lost its head, with a crown collar. This signifies that she was a member of the Court of King Richard II. When Mr Cole visited the Church in 1757, he commented:

"round the neck of one of these knights I observed that a fresh garland of flowers and was informed that an estate was held by the tenure of putting such a chaplet every year about this on the said tomb." [6]

The flowers would have been on Dame Isabel not on the knight. This goes back to a grant of land by Roger la Zouche in 1200. One of the conditions was:

"Rendering yearly to the said Roger and his heirs a chaplet of roses upon the feast day of the nativity of St John the Baptist in case he or they shall be at Tonge, if not then to be put upon the image of the blessed Virgin in the Church of Tonge."

So a custom over 200 years old, continued into the new church. But at the Reformation, the statue of Our Lady would have been removed, and so the roses came to the other lady, who was lying near the Lady Chapel. The custom still continues today. Such customs were common practice. In 1316, John de Tong was granted land by Robert de Prees; the rent was a rose on Midsummer's Day. In 1353 there was a grant by John Byschop of 3 pieces of land at Tong Norton, with a similar arrangement. Another grant was conditional on the exchange of three arrows with goose feathers. [7]

At the base of the tomb are heraldic shields. Dugdale, visiting the Church in 1663, was able to record them. Tests done in 1982 confirmed his findings, but there is little to see now. [8]

Lion at Sir Richard Vernon's feet

2) Opposite is the tomb of Sir Richard Vernon and Benedicta de Ludlow. Gardner considers this as: *"one of the finest and most imposing of all alabaster knights that have come down to us."* [9] It is also very well preserved. Around the base are angels holding shields, alternating with the twelve apostles, each holding their traditional symbol. Sir Richard is in elaborate armour. His helmet incorporates the boar's head, which is the Vernon family crest. Benedicta has a mitred head-dress. Small scraps of paint are still visible on both these tombs.

3) To the west, is Sir William Vernon. This is a fine brass, inlaid in Purbeck marble. It depicts Sir William, his wife and their ten children (including two sets of twins). Tradition has it that Sir William was engaged in some local skirmish, and returned home, mortally wounded. He made his will, and asked to be buried in Tong Church. Masses would have been said on this altar tomb. William required that a priest would *"sing thereat for three years".*

Anne (Talbot) Vernon

4) The Chantry Chapel contains the tomb of Henry Vernon and his wife. This tomb is made of stone. The tomb is contained within a Burgundian Arch. Above it are canopies, which would have contained figures of saints. Some of the carving is very delicate. Anne Talbot has the Talbot dog at her feet. The whole Chantry is remarkable with its fan

vaulting ceiling, which was originally painted in green, red and gold. The vaulting is very like that in the Henry VII Chapel in Westminster Abbey. The size of the Tong Chapel is much smaller, what could be achieved is restricted. It is the only surviving piece of medieval fan vaulting in Shropshire. On the east wall are the remains of a rood painting. Some of the colour is still quite bright. Underneath is an inscription requesting prayers for Henry Vernon and his family. On the west wall, there is a hollow bust of Arthur Vernon, depicted in a pulpit, preaching. On the floor is a fine brass of Arthur Vernon dressed as an Oxford M.A. Arthur was Henry's third son, tutor to Prince Arthur and subsequently Rector of Whitchurch. Recent research by Heather Gilderdale Scott points out that this chapel:

"Through its stylistic repertoire it aligns itself with some of the finest contemporary building projects whilst its more innovative aspects appear in turn to have been emulated by others"

She then goes on to makes some very interesting comparisons between Henry Vernon's chapel and that of his patron and friend King Henry VII in Westminster Abbey. [10]

Ceiling of the Golden Chapel

We noted in Chapter 4 that George Durant turned this into his family pew. The chapel was panelled, and, in doing this, he cut the front off the piscina and boarded in the Aumbry (for the Reserved Sacrament), which was on the east wall. At the Victorian restoration, when the panelling was removed, the Aumbry was found to contain the remains of a loaf of bread. [11] The stone altar slab, with its consecration crosses, was found on the floor, and restored to its proper place. A collection of tiles from various places were put on the altar step. [12]

5) As well as Arthur Vernon, two other of Henry's sons are buried in Tong Church. At the far side in the Lady Chapel, is an incised marble tomb to Humphrey Vernon of Hodnet (died 1542 or 45) By the pulpit is the tomb of Henry's heir, Richard Vernon and his wife Margaret Dymoke. He was very young, when he died in 1517, only two years after his father. The lower part of this tomb was removed, at one period, to provide a front for the High Altar and only put back in 1892. On the west end of the tomb is a depiction of their son, George Vernon, who lived at Haddon. Thus at Tong, there are the only depictions that exist of six generations of the Vernons (if you include the Stanley Tomb). This is only matched by the Manners family tombs at Bottesford.

Henry's son, Roger, is not buried at Tong. Roger had been involved in the forced abduction and marriage to the heiress Margaret Kebell in 1502, (for which the Vernons were heavily fined by the king); but he died in 1509, before his father. [13]

The question has been raised as to why the Vernons, who also owned Haddon Hall, used Tong as their Chantry and burial place. The answer seems to be that Bakewell Parish Church was not an option for the Vernons, because they did not take over the Manor of Bakewell until 1498. At that time, there was no chapel at Haddon Hall. The tradition of burying at Tong, with its Chantry and a College, to pray for the dead, was by then well established. [14]

6) The Stanley Tomb requires much closer consideration because of its literary connections. It originally stood on the north side of the High Altar. It was moved from there by George Durant (II) to make way for his father's memorial. This was removed at the 1892 restoration. There are drawings showing the tomb, lying parallel with the east wall of the north aisle, and barred by railings. At the Victorian restoration the tomb was realigned on an east-west axis.

<u>Drawing of Stanley tomb before the 1892 restoration</u>

On the top of this very elaborate tomb, are the effigies of Sir Thomas Stanley and his wife (Margaret Vernon). Underneath is the effigy of Sir Edward Stanley. As originally designed, the four pillars had golden balls on the top, and carved figures at each corner (some of these figures are now in the Burgundian Arch to the Golden Chapel). At each end of the tomb, are words attributed to Shakespeare (see Chapter 12).

Along one side is a summary the Stanley family. This reads:

"Thomas Stanley, Second Soon of Edward Earl of Derbie, Lord Stanley and Strange Descended From The Familie of The Stanleys Married Margaret Vernon one Of The daughters And Cohairs of Sir George Vernon Of Nethher Haddon In the Countie Of Derbie Knight. By Whom He Has Issue Two Soons Henri and Edw: Henrie Dyed An Infant. E Survived to Whoom Thos Lordships Descended And Married the La: Lucie Percie Second Daughter of Tho: Percie Of Northumberland By Her He Had Issue 7 Daughters and One Soone Shee And Her 4 Daughters 18 Arabella 16 Marie 15 Alice and 13 Priscilla Are Interred Under a Monument In Ye Churche Of Waltham In Ye Countie of Essex. Thomas His Soone Dyed In His Infancie & Is Buried In Ye Parish Church of Winwicke In Ye Countie Of Lancs: Ye Other Three Petronella, Francis, And Venise Are Yet Livinge".

When the floor of the Sanctuary was raised in 1892, the lead coffin of Sir Thomas Stanley was found. The lid to his coffin had these words in Latin:

"Here lies Thomas Stanley, knight, second son of Edward, Earl of Derby and husband of Margaret and one of the heiress of George Vernon Knight who died on 21st day of December in the 19th year of our Lord 1576. One whose soul may God have mercy. Amen. Done by me John Latham".

There was also a small lead box from which the contents had been removed. [15] This may have contained Margaret Vernon's heart. She had asked to be buried at Tong, but finally was not. Margaret married Sir Thomas Stanley in 1558.

When Sir Thomas's son, Edward, was born, the Earl of Derby drew up an agreement, whereby certain properties were left to Sir Thomas, and thereafter to his son, Edward. When his father died, Edward was only 14. He was not free to sell Tong, until the death of his grandfather in 1603. So in 1603, Edward sold three of his properties including Tong, which came into the hands of Sir Thomas Harries. (Harries was Shropshire man who became Sergeant at Law in 1589, knighted in 1603 and made a baronet in 1523. He was MP for various Parliamentary seats between 1584 and 1601.)

Edward Stanley eventually moved to Eynsham. (The Earls of Derby had owned Eynsham Abbey since 1545). He was there in 1615, and buried there in 1632. [16] Reference on the side of the tomb to *"Waltham"* and the fact four of his daughters and his wife are buried there implies that the family there for some time. All three of them died in 1601, possibly of a contagious disease. But *"Waltham"* has confused people. The tomb to his widow and daughters is in St Mary's Church, Walthamstow, not at Waltham Abbey, as previously assumed. The Walthamstow tomb looks as if it may have been made by the same tomb maker, at the same time as the Tong one. The words on the Walthamstow tomb are very similar. [17] Sir Edward never remarried.

Uncertainty over the question of when the tomb was erected, has led to much confusion. It seems most likely that the tomb was erected after 1601. Mrs Esdaile thinks the tomb was made at Southwark, probably by the second William Crump, but proposed a date of 1612 for its manufacture. [18] But she thought Tong was sold twenty years later, in 1623. More importantly, the antiquarian and friend of Shakespeare, John Weever states that Sir Edward told him that he erected his Tomb, while he was still alive. [19] Edward may have made it expecting to be buried at Tong. It only depicts himself; so it was after his wife's death. She was dead before Edward decided to sell Tong. This implies that the tomb was erected before the end of 1602.

MEMORIALS

As well as the tombs, there are many other memorials that tell more of the story of Tong

1) **Anne Wylde**. A monument on the south wall of the sanctuary is a fine depiction of Anne Wylde. She was the eldest daughter of Sir Thomas Harries, and married John Wylde of Droitwich. She died in childbirth, at the age of 16. It was her sister who married William Pierrepoint. The end of the monument reads:

"Short was my life the longer is my rest
God takes them soonest whom he loveth best
For he that's borne today and dyes tomorrow
Looseth some days of Joy but months of sorrow
Then cease dear Infant, Husband, Parents, Friends
To wale my woes, in heaven I have amends"

2) **Henry Willoughby**. His monument is on the floor of the sanctuary. He was the youngest son of Lord Middleton and rented Tong Castle from the Duke of Kingston and died there in 1742. At the restoration of the

Church his vault was opened and found to contain just one single coffin. The family motto was *Truth without Fear".*

3) **Elizabeth Pierrepoint**. Over the door to the Vestry is a complex memorial in two parts. The top part is the bust of a lady, who might be Elizabeth Harries. [20] Underneath, is the memorial to the daughter of the Duke of Kingston, who died at the age of 11 in 1697. The words reveal a deeply grieving Duke, and ends (in Greek) with the words *"He whom the Gods love dies young".*

4) **Skeffington**. These memorials in two parts separated by the previous memorial were removed from the east wall at some point. One is the memorial of William Skeffington of White Ladies, who died in 1550. The other is of his mother, Lady Daunsey. She died in 1549, so it likely both memorials were installed at the same time. In Brewood Church, there is a memorial to Joan Levison. She married William Skeffington, and, after his death, married Edward Giffard of Chillington.

5) **Buckeridge**. Above the Choir stalls, on the north side, is a memorial to Charles Buckeridge, a Durant cousin, who ended up as Archdeacon of Coventry. Also commemorated is his second wife, Elizabeth Slaney and three children. She came from a noted Shropshire family. They are all interred in a vault under the Vestry floor.

6) **Higgs**. Over the door to the Chantry is a memorial to Daniel Higgs who was the Duke of Kingston's agent. He died (aged 60) in 1758. The bottom inscription reads *"Few so honest. None more so".* Opposite, is the memorial to his daughter Maria Higgs who died (aged 19) in 1748.

7) **Randalph Elcock**. This refurbished brass in the south wall of the nave commemorates a cellarer of the College who died in 1510.

8) **John Boden**. This brass plaque, situated on the tower pillar near the organ, is the only one to a Parish Clerk. We shall read of the activities of his son in Chapter 13.

9) **Durant**. There are three Durant memorials. The very large marble memorial to George Durant (I) is fixed, uneasily, on the east side of the north tower pillar. There is a debate about who designed it. It may be by Chantry, but Pevsner attributes it to John Bacon. His son erected it in the Sanctuary. There are ten Durant coffins in the vault under the chancel floor. George (I) is described as follows:

His sentiments were liberal
His dispositions humane
His manners polished
Happy alike in his mental
As in his personal accomplishments.

This is a strange description of a man, who had several affairs, cooked the army books, and took part in the slave trade. It may express the way his son would like to be seen himself. Underneath in smaller letters is a later addition referring to the daughter Maria who died at the age of 4. Also to George (II)'s son Mark (who was drowned), and the daughter, Emma, (who is buried in Paris). George describes himself as *"Her disconsolate father"*.

There are two other Durant memorials, which are on the wall at the east end of the north aisle. One lists the death of the children of George (II) first marriage ending with reference to his mother's death at Dawlish and his first wife's death at Seighford. The other lists the death of children of his second marriage and ends with his own death. The last entry is that of Ernest in 1846. This may be the date of the inscriptions, as they are all in the same lettering.

The Sanctuary used to contain two Durant hatchment shields, which were carried in front of the coffin at the funeral. [21] The final Durant memorial in the Church is a large Royal Coat of Arms made of Coadware (a mixture of glass and sand) fixed on the north side of the Nave. It was put in to commemorate the Peace of Paris of 1814. It is above a bricked up doorway, which is known as *"The door of excommunication"*. This is the door through which people who were excommunicated had to leave the church.

Outside, there is another Durant memorial. It is in the gap between the north aisle and the Vestry, in a space known as "Chrysom's Graveyard". It contains a large Maltese cross made of red sandstone and containing (now indecipherable) verses by Thomas Moore (his favourite poet), Walter Scott and Byron. The Scott lines at the bottom read:

"Like the last beam of evening thrown
On a white cloud– just seen and gone".

Durant used this space for the burial of his own unbaptised children. But before the Reformation a "Chrysom child" was one who was baptised, but died early, and who at death still had the crysom cloth around their head. The cloth was placed there after the priest anointed the child at baptism. It had to be worn for a week after the baptism. Following an emergency baptism the cloth would still be in place.

10) **Bridgeman**. By the south door are memorials to the Bridgeman family – the new owner of Tong, the Earls of Bradford, though their main memorials are at Weston under Lizard.

11) **Sir Charles Mander**. There is a memorial to Sir Charles Mander of Kilsall (see Chapter 10), who was churchwarden for many years. He also paid for the mechanism to chime the bells.

WAR MEMORIALS

There are two war memorials, which name more ordinary Tong people. The First World War Memorial has 12 names (quite small from a population of over 500). Half of them were under twenty, and three aged over 30. Some familiar names appear, like Boden, Beech and Rowley. They were all soldiers.

There are only three names from the Second World War. The RAF officer, Mark Hastings, lived at the Red House.

PERSONAL INCISIONS

The choir stalls are covered with the initials of choirboys from over the years. Inside the screen in the south Aisle is a very striking carving in Tudor style of the name "JOHN BABYN". In the window at the west end of the south Aisle is a piece of glass inscribed with the words *Elizabeth Davenport 1672*. Most interesting of all, are three rough crosses on the outside wall at the east end of the South Aisle. An old notebook comments:

"There are those for whom this place is hallowed ground, they used to come and kneeling, pray for the souls of their departed kinsfolk and friends".

This is an example of how folk religion prevails over theological niceties. The inside of this wall would have been where the altar for Requiem Masses would have been. When requiems were abolished at the Reformation the people just prayed outside.

OUTSIDE THE CHURCH

The community always makes itself felt in the Churchyard. There are many eighteenth century memorials. The members of the Durant family, who were not approved of, as a result of family feuds, are buried round a tree near the edge of the Churchyard. There are memorials to several owners of Ruckley Grange, including the very large walled in space, for Mr Reid Walker. The Hartleys, tenants of Tong Castle, are buried at the east end, but there are also many farmers, local residents and schoolteachers, but very few of the clergy. Four leading members of the community died in the summer of 1976. This was, in part, due to the great heat of that summer.

Niche figure of St. Bartholomew

At the middle of the churchyard is an old preaching cross, which was turned into a sundial by Thomas Ore, one of the Tong Clockmakers. A modern sculpture of St Bartholomew holding the church can be seen on the north-east corner of the Church. Mrs Pat Austin made it, in the 1960s. She is the wife of the well-known Albrighton rose-grower. There used to be a face carved out of stone in a tree near the gate, but it was stolen.

THE RESTORATION OF TONG CHURCH

The Church gives the impression of being a single unity. It is hard to tell where alterations have been made. The central tower was altered to house the Great Bell and this may have taken place at the same time that the Golden Chapel was added. Standing on the roof, you can see an earlier roof level. Before 1886, the only alterations seem to have been to the Golden Chapel and the move of the Stanley Tomb.

Old prints show the church with box pews, a three-decker pulpit, and all at one level. Mr Petit, writing in 1845, pointed out that a restoration could not be long delayed:

"It is hardly to be supposed that so beautiful a church will long escape the process of restoration. Nor indeed it is altogether wished, though I should earnestly deprecate it on a very comprehensive scale. Externally some of the pinnacles are broken or displaced, and others have lost their finials; if these were renewed after the model of such as are sufficiently perfect to preserve their general effect, the latter being suffered to remain untouched, and other mutilations of stone work, as in the tracery of the West window, carefully repaired,

no doubt the general aspect would be improved. The same applies to the woodwork of the interior. Some of the poppy heads that have slightly suffered from decay, might be preserved in their present state, others might be restored, and the barbarous work with which a few of them have been repaired, I suppose during the last or preceding century, might be replaced with work of better character. The repairs of the rood screen would require careful and able artists, but in this it would be desirable to remove none of the present work that can possible be kept in place. In the nave several unsightly pews rise above the level of the original seats, and might be removed with great advantage to the appearance of the building. The original disposition of the seats does not seem to have been disturbed except in one or two instances and could easily have been required for the wants of the parish. The monuments admit of some repair, there being several fractures, especially in the most beautiful one No 12 (Sir Richard Vernon). Some stoves, too, that are in the body of the church, by no means conducive to its beauty; and I would further suggest that if the Golden Chapel must be used as a pew some tapestry of the date and character of the sixteenth century, might advantageously replace the present linings and curtains of cloth and some good cinquecento paned glass be substituted for the modern coloured panes in its windows." [22]

Clearly the church was in a bit of a mess, but these were tumultuous times at Tong. In the following year, George Durant (II) died, and the Castle was sold nine years later. Any restoration would be the responsibility of the new Lay Rector (The Earl of Bradford). It was not until 1887 that the Vicar began to look into question of restoration. He asked the architect, George Street, to help. Street had built a fine new Church at St George's Pains Lane (now part of Telford) in 1861, and restored Blymhill Church (also in the gift of Lord Bradford) between 1856 and 1869. Street recommended stripping the plaster off the walls. We hear no more of George Street, and the person finally appointed to supervise the work was Ewan Christian. He was the Church Commissioners' architect, and had been responsible for the restoration of St Peter's Wolverhampton (1852-65) and of Lord Bradford's church at Weston under Lizard (1876-7). The repairs to Tong Church cost between £4 - 5,000.

The work was phased over several years. In 1886-7, the upper part of the spire was found to be decayed, and the pinnacles and parapets of the tower were in danger of collapse. The repairs were done, and the weathercock was replaced (One of the Durant sons had shot at the previous one.) The lead gutters were replaced. In the following year, the pinnacles of the Nave and Chancel were restored. The oak roofs were taken down, and decayed timbers replaced. The Shrewsbury Chronicle commented:

"While the scaffolding was up inside, it was taken advantage of to remove the many coatings of colour and whiting which had been superimposed upon it during many generations, revealing the stone walls. Thus once more being found to be beautiful in the face and tone." [23]

The Victorians thought that mediaeval churches were meant to have stone walls. They were not. The mention of colour on the wall is disturbing, and it hints that there may have been murals of some sort. Griffiths says that there was a small patch of an ancient mural. [24]

New drainage was put around the outside of the Church, and the floor of the Chancel was raised. This revealed many of the internments underneath. The Choir Stalls and the screens were mended and had new carving inserted.

The next task was the Nave. A new cement floor was laid and covered with new red tiles. The old pews with some alterations were refixed. Of the three-decker pulpit, only the actual pulpit was retained, without its sounding board. A new heating system was installed, operated from a boiler house some 50 yards from the Church. This remained in use until the mid 1970s, but was inefficient because there was a massive heat loss before it reached the Church. New doors were installed at the west end, and the Golden Chapel restored. The Great Bell was recast and rehung.

The Church was re-opened on 23rd June 1892 when the preacher was the Bishop of Lichfield (Rt. Revd and Hon Augustus Legge).

Various discoveries were made during the restoration, (most of which have been noted). Two old silver coins were found, and a small slab, which still to be seen in the north aisle, seems to represent a priest with the following letters still visible *LE WARDE   ERC J*. It may refer to a Warden of Tong College. Various other tombstones were discovered and recorded. [25]

So Tong Church revealed some of its secrets. The new Lord of the Manor made his mark by his munificence, and the Durant era put in its context. Tong Church remains the most valuable social document of the community.

NOTES

[1] See **Some Notes on Shottesbrooke Church**. The Victorian architect J. Butterfield wrote a detailed analysis of the building in 1847.
[2] N. Pevsner **Shropshire**
[3] Petrie
[4] For an article on he Lily crucifix see B. Harris **Guide to Churches and Cathedrals** pp338-341
[5] For details see A. Gardner **Alabaster Tombs.** Very similar tombs, of the Manners family can be seen in Bottesford Church, Leicestershire. See E. Shipman **Gleanings about the Church of St Mary Bottesford** and also his guidebook to the Church.
[6] **The Gentleman's Magazine** 1757
[7] See papers at Belvoir Castle
[8] A. Hulbert's report
[9] A. Gardner pp58
[10] H. Gilderdale Scott **This Little Westminster The Chantry Chapel of Sir Henry Vernon at Tong Shropshire**.
[11] Cranage
[12] A. Wharton **The Tiles in Tong Church**
[13] Article in ODNB
[14] Prof. A. Cox **Comments on J. E. Auden's Notes on Tong**
[15] George Griffiths **The Restoration of Tong Church**
[16] L. Wright **The Stanleys in Eynsham**
[17] See S. Watney **Sky Aspiring Pyramids**. See there for the slightly different wording on the Walthamstow monument, which may imply that it is earlier. The words on the Walthamstow tomb reads:

"Tho Stanley, Knight, Second Sonne of Edw./Earle of Derbie, Lo: Stanley & Strange/descended from Ye Familie Of Ye Stanlies,/Married Margaret Vernon One of Ye Daughters/and Coheirs if Sir George Vernon of Nether/ Haddon In Ye Countie Of Derbie, Knight, By/Whom He Had Issue 2 Sonnes Henrie And /Edw: Henrie Died An Infant: Edw: Survived/To Whoome The Lordshipe Descended &/ Married La:Lucie Percie Second-Daugh/Ter Of The Earl of Northumberland By Her/He had Issue 7 Daughters & One Sonne: She & He 4 daughters Arbella Marie, Alis And Pricilla Are Interred Under a monument/In the Church of Walthamstow In The Countie Of Essex Tho: His Sonne Died an/Infant &Is Buried."

[18] Mrs Esdaile **Shakespeare's Verses in Tong Church**
[19] E.A.J. Honigmann **John Weever**
[20] According to George Griffiths
[21] Ibid
[22] Petit quoted in **The Archaeological Journal**
[23] **The Shrewsbury Chronicle**
[24] See 15 above
[25] Ibid

The Tong Cup

Chapter 8
The Treasures of Tong

Just as every home has its treasured objects, so does Tong Church, and they reveal some more about community life.

THE GREAT BELL OF TONG

Camden, the topographer, writing in 1590 reported that:

"The inhabitants if Tong boast of nothing more at present than the Great Bell, famous in these parts for its bigness." [1]

Similarly Elihu Burritt wrote:

"The great bell hung on the rudest frame in the tower is a rival in size and weight to the Big Tom of Lincoln or the mellow thunderer of Westminster. It could never have been turned on its concentric axis without throwing down the steeple." [2]

The Bell tells its own story. Inscribed on it (in Latin) are the following statements:

Henry Vernon, Knight, caused this bell to be made 1518 to the glory of God Almighty, the Blessed Mary and St Bartholomew. Which having been broken through the madness of enemies was recast at the expense of the parish Ab Rudhall Gloucester, in the year 1720. L. Pietier, minister. T. Woodshaw, T. Peynten, Churchwardens.

Orlando George Charles, Earl of Bradford, took care that this same bell, now cracked with age should be cast anew and replaced. John Courtney Clarke Vicar 1892.

In his will, Henry Vernon instructed the bells to be installed to be rung by the Church deacons to signal the start and close of the religious day and to augment the celebration of Daily Mass in the College. He paid for it by income from the Manor of Norton. It originally weighed 2 tons and 18cwt and measured six yards round. It is the largest bell in Shropshire. It normally takes three people to toll it.

The Bell was broken during the Civil War, around 1643, but not recast until 1720. This was a matter of local controversy. The Churchwardens did not call the required Parish Meeting, but ordered the casting of a treble bell. Many parishioners refused to pay the rate; so the wardens then commissioned the recasting of the Great Bell. This was a legal charge on the church rate. The treble bell was inscribed *Peace and Good Neighbourhood AR*

1719. Auden dryly comments that whoever chose this motto had a sense of humour!

The Bell was cracked again on Ash Wednesday 1848, and not recast until 1892. The Bell now weighs 50cwt. (or 2.5 metric Tonnes). For many years, the Bell may not have been rung at all. There was also anxiety that so big a bell might threaten the structure of the Tower. Thus, in 1892, the Vicar and churchwardens laid down rules for its tolling, only on certain occasions:

When a member of the Royal Family or the head of the Vernon family visits Tong.

On the birth of an heir to the Earldom of Bradford, and when a new incumbent is instituted.

On the following Church festivals: Christmas Day, Easter Day, Whitsunday and St Bartholomew's Day.

The Bell is to be tolled to mark the deaths of the Monarch, the Bishop of Lichfield, the Vicar of Tong, and the Earl of Bradford. It is also to be tolled on Good Friday. [3]

The booming of the Great Bell echoes all over the village. Thus it tells part of the Village story. To this day, a member of the Vernon family, or of the Royal Family does visit occasionally. The tolling of the Bell is a sign of continuity, over five centuries.

OTHER BELLS

Above the Great Bell, are a peal of six, and a Sanctus Bell. This last, used at the Elevation of the Host in the Mass, was given by Sir William Vernon, in 1467. The other bells date between 1593 and 1810. The old tenor bell was recast in 1810. The oldest bell was donated by William Fitzherbert in 1451 [4]. When the bell was recast, some fragments of the Great Bell were used. During the casting, in London, Mrs Chapman (widow of George Durant I) threw into the molten metal an apron, full of old silver items. When the bell arrived back at Tong, it was tipped upside down. It was filled with old Ale from the Castle, and a drunken orgy ensued.

The Sanctus Bell was known as TING TONG. One Sunday in the 1860s, the Parish Clerk could not get it to ring. One of the bell ringers had muffled it. A few Sundays later, the same ringer was ringing the tenor bell, and the rope fell on him. Someone had cut it. *"I should like to know who has done this,"* said the ringer. The Parish Clerk replied *"The same man who muffled the ting-tong".*

Auden came across an old sampler, worked by Lucy Wooley (1810-1875) of Tong Forge. The words had been written by Thomas Cherrington:

"LINES ON TONG BELLS

The first sounds sweet and charming, the second sharp and shrill,
The third is like temptation unto a tender will,
The fourth rings clear like silver; the fifth for service chimes;
The tenor bids us ponder sorrows darkest times.
Let solemn thoughts engage our minds
Our wondering Francis fix.
Whenever we hear our Tong bells go
One, two three, four five six."

Bell ringers are always a community within a community. They have a rather distinct view of life. Calling people to worship, they rarely worship themselves: and they are rather addicted to rules and regulations. The Tong ringers look as if they were no different. They had their own Ringer's Carol, printed in a book of hymns for use in Tong Church, in 1828. Nor were they concerned about the church fabric. Parts of the Vernon tomb have come off, because the ringers tied their ropes to it.

There is also a notice board giving rules for the bell ringers. It implies that the ringers might drink and swear a lot. It is dated 1694. At one time, the Bishop of Lichfield ordered it to be removed; because he thought it was unseemly.

"If that to Ring you do come here,
you must ring well with hand and eare.
keep stroak of time and goe not out:
or else you forfeit out of doubt.
Our law is so concluded here;
for every fault a jugg of beer,
If that you ring with Spurr or Hat:
a jugg of beer must pay for that,
If that you take a Rope in hand;
these forfeits you must not withstand,
Or if that you a bell ov'rthrow;
it must cost Sixpence e're you goe,
If in this place you sweare or curse;
Sixpence to pay, pull out your purse.
come pay the Clerk it is his fee;

for one (that swears) shall not goe free,
These Laws are old, and are not new;
therefore the Clerk must have his due.
GEO HARISON 1694

CHURCH MUSIC

The present organ was installed in 1877. It was made by Walker and Co, and is adequate for the building. This was just the next step in the history of church music at Tong.

The 1411 Statutes of Tong College required that on special days the High Mass must be:

"celebrated with double or triple music according as that music is attached these days. The antiphons are to be sung with music at every service."

There might have been a small Gothic organ to assist the music. If there had been, it would have been situated in the Rood Loft. The Loft was not removed until the eighteenth century. An account of 1789 states:

"The gallery, with the entrance to the choir, is as yet unremoved, and the organ case remains, with little more room than was sufficient for the player. This organ, to judge by what is left, seems the most ancient of the sort that has come under my observation, which for the entertainment of your musical-mechanical readers, I will describe. And first, the case. It is a true Gothic, with pinnacles and finials after the manner of ancient tabernacles and very like the one just finished and erected in Lichfield cathedral, only on a smaller scale. Now, as to the other parts, the keys are gone, but the sounding board remains, and is pierced for one set of pipes only, seemingly an open diapason, whether of metal or wood could not be determined, there not being a single pipe left; from the apparent position and distance I presume they were of metal. I perceived no registers or slide for other stops, and observed the compass to be very short— only to A in alto for the treble part, and short octaves in the lower bass; therefore not more than forty tones on the whole. The bellows were preserved in a lumber-room near the vestry, double winded without folds, and made with thick hides. Like unto a smith's or forge bellows. Thus simply constructed there could be no transmutation of sounding pipes, not that variation to be produced from a mixture of different flute and reed pipes." [5]

This gives an impression of a church, filled with junk. We do not know when it was all removed. For a period, following the custom of the time, a Village band replaced the organ. It performed in the choir stalls and marks can be seen on the stalls where the music stands were fixed. Auden says that he found two books in the vestry entitled *"Church Harmony, sacred to devotion being a choice set of new anthems and psalm tunes on various subjects".* He thought that they dated from the early nineteenth century. They gave the parts for the instruments. Thomas Ore played the clarinet.

By 1810, the Church had a barrel organ. The tunes for the service were installed, by the Parish Clerk, before the service. One Sunday in the 1840s, someone inserted an old popular song *"Moll in the Wad and I fell out, and what do you think it was about"* (This was an old Irish jig and may refer to the Lady in the Lake). As the Clerk turned the handle, in Auden's words *"this utterly secular tune pealed forth, to the utter consternation of many of the congregation, and to the great amusement of the rest."*

A small organ, from Lichfield Cathedral, replaced the barrel organ. This was placed in the Chancel, on the north-east end of the stalls near to the Vestry door. Concerts were given to raise money for a new organ. The 1877 Organ was moved to its present position in 1892.

Music changes to meet patterns of worship, but it is often difficult for small rural parishes to find an organist. Changes in the community can affect the availability of a choir. When Lord Bradford disposed of his flock of sheep, the Choir was halved in size. The shepherd had five children! There are now the Tong Singers, who sing on special occasions. As more people learn musical instruments, it is possible that the Tong Church Band might re-emerge.

THE EASTER SEPULCHRE

One of the things that Tong has in common with Shottesbrooke is the Easter Sepulchre. They are both placed on the north side of the sanctuary. At Tong, it was turned in to a cupboard when the Sanctuary was panelled in the 1892 restoration. The 1451 will of William Fitzherbert refers to a legacy of 3s 4d *'To the new Sepulchre at Tong.'*[6] This may imply that it was a feature imported into the new Church from Shottesbrooke.

The Easter Sepulchre is a strange aspect of the rather confused liturgical history of Holy Week. The earliest reference to it is in the **Concordia Regularis** of St Dunstan. Following the veneration of the Cross on Good Friday, the cross was placed in the sepulchre and a watch kept until Easter Sunday morning. After the third responsory at Matins, three priests would approach the sepulchre slowly as if they were looking for something. The Choir sang the words *"Whom do you seek"*. The curtain from the front of the sepulchre was lifted and the cross was shown to have gone while the choir sang *"Christ is Risen"*. The clergy bring out a linen shroud showing that Christ had indeed risen. At a later period when there was more emphasis on the sacrament, the priest would consecrate two extra hosts on Maundy Thursday. One would be used for the Mass of the Pre-Sanctified on Good Friday and the final one was placed in the sepulchre with the cross.

A pattern of worship like this was followed in the Sarum Rite, which was used at Tong College. In modern times the Easter Sepulchre has been replaced by the Easter Garden. There is little doubt that the ceremonies surrounding the Easter Sepulchre were very dramatic. It is good to be reminded of this part of the Church's liturgical history.

THE TONG MINISTER'S LIBRARY

In the Eighteenth Century, the growth of literacy and increased availability of printed books, led to the establishment of Minister's Libraries. This was to enable clergy to have access to books, which they could ill afford to buy. The man behind this movement was Dr Thomas Bray. He was the founder of both the Society for the Propagation of the Gospel (SPG) and the Society for the Promotion of Christian Knowledge (SPCK). Bray was a Shropshire man, born at Chirbury in 1658; and ordained in 1681. In 1697, he proposed the establishment of Parochial Libraries. [7] There were seven such Libraries in Shropshire. [8] The Library at Tong was one of the earliest, and established by the Duke of Kingston. At that time, he was mourning the death of his 11 year old daughter. He founded several other local charities in the same period.

The Deed for the Library reads:

"For the better accommodation of the Minister and his successors, the trustees should at the decease of the said Lord Pierrepoint, hold and enjoy for ever one chamber in the aforesaid Castle of Tong, the uppermost chamber up the back stairs there, as the same was then furnished with books and presses on both sides, together with the usual free and uninterrupted ways or passage to and from it, and also the free and full use of all the said books, and all such others as the Lord Pierrepoint should, during his life appropriate to the use of the minister and his successors; and the seventeenth century useful library of reference by a nobleman who as patron of the living, gave his books to the clergyman he sat under, and also what was that clergyman's own private reading." [9]

The original catalogue was written on parchment. [10] Later, a printed catalogue was compiled by Beriah Botfield. The Duke presented 369

Portrait of George Durant (I) by Sir Joshua Reynolds (1762)

Belle Isle – George Durant II's watercolour sketchbook

Convent Lodge – George Durant II's watercolour sketchbook

White Oak Lodge – George Durant II's watercolour sketchbook

Knowle Hall – George Durant II's watercolour sketchbook

The Hermitage – George Durant II's watercolour sketchbook

volumes; these included a number of medical textbooks, dating between 1649 and 1700. The Duke had collected these, in a desperate attempt to find a cure for his sick daughter. The oldest book was a volume (no 193), which belonged to Catherine of Aragon. [11] There is an old volume on the Councils of the Early Church. Lewis Peitier (Vicar 1695-1745) added 77 books of his own.

When the Duke built the Vicarage, the Library was moved from the Castle. But because of absentee Vicars, it was moved into the Church Vestry and a fireplace installed. George Durant (II), and the Revd T. Buckeridge, added some other books. During the 1892 restoration the Vicar checked the volumes against Botfield's Catalogue. He discovered that it contained 409 books, of which 89 were missing. There were 70 books not included in the Catalogue. Having found some volumes from the Library in a second-hand book cart in Wolverhampton, Auden did a further check. Clearly pilfering was rife.

The books remained in a muddle until the 1960s. At this time Church Authorities were being concerned about the amount of archive material in parish churches, which was not being properly conserved. The two Shropshire Archdeacons arranged for all the Parochial Libraries to be properly deposited in the Shropshire County Archives. There were 554 volumes from Tong. [12] Some books were in several volumes, which in part, explains the discrepancy in the numbers. The books have all been properly catalogued, and many rebound.

THE ELIZABETHAN PUPLIT FALL

A great benefactor of the Church was Dame Elinor Harries (died 1635), the wife of Sir Thomas Harries. Her father was Roger (or Robert) Giffard of Chillington, who was physician to Queen Elizabeth I. As well as the Tong Cup (see below) she left:

"a yewer and plate of silver. A cloth for the communion table of diaper; the pulpitt; a clothe and cushion of velvet worked with silver for the Pulpitt; a pulpitt clothe of blacke onely for funeral sermonts; a black clothe to cover the biere at all burials." [13]

She also donated the fine Jacobean pulpit. The silver ewer (which is in the Victoria and Albert Museum) has a hall mark of 1606 and is described as:

"a silver round-bellied flagon, with dragon-headed spout, standing 12and a half inches high."

The paten is dated 1627-8 and has the Harries shield on it. The pulpit bears the inscription *"Ex dono Dom. Harries 1629"*. The other cloths no longer exist, but the pulpit fall is in a glass case in the vestry. It is described by George Griffiths:

"In a glass case is an ancient dalmatic or ecclesiastical VESTMENT of red velvet, embroidered and ornamental in gold and coloured silks with cherubs in raised work, flowers and other devices and four scrolls of which two bear mottos:

1) Cor Unum Via (one heart, one way)

and   2) Use bein Temps (Use time well)

It is considered a beautiful specimen of needlework, and is supposed to have been made by the Nuns at the Cloisters of St. Leonard of the Cistercian order for use in their chapel (now called Whiteladies, and in ruins, a mile or to from Tong). It is said to be 300 years old. It was given by Lady Harries and to a late period used as a pulpit frontal. Size about six feet square." [14]

Here, we see the way myths develop. Griffiths was quoting from a notebook by the Revd R. G. Lawrence (Vicar 1870-76). Lawrence was an early Tractarian, and clearly wanted to introduce Eucharistic vestments to Tong. So he used the pulpit fall to justify this innovation. The 1630 Churchwardens accounts simply describe it as a pulpit fall. The first motto is that of the Cecil family. Lord Burleigh was high treasurer to Queen Elizabeth I. The other is the motto of the Giffard family, Roger Giffard was her Physician. It may denote a connection between the two families.

THE TONG CUP

An even more complex story surrounds this Cup, described in the accounts as *"A Communion Cup of goulde and christall"*. This must be Tong's greatest treasure. It has been variously attributed. Pevsner dates it between 1540 and 1550, which is far too early. [15] He and Griffiths attribute its design to Holbein. Griffiths says it is a sacramental vessel from the time of King Henry VIII and belonged to Tong College. He thought it was a ciborium for holding communion wafers. Cranage says it was a monstrance for displaying the reserved sacrament. Auden speculates that it might have belonged to the College, removed at the Dissolution, and given back later.

The cup stands 11 inches high. It is decorated with vine leaves and grapes. Set in the middle is a piece of carved Crystal. This is held in place by clasps, with lion's heads on them. It is made of silver gilt, and has no markings to provide details of its provenance, or maker. All we know is that it came to Tong in 1630. This is itself a clue. There are four other pieces made by the same hand; one is in the Victoria & Albert Museum (dated 1611), and three are at Corpus Christi College, Cambridge. A cup, of very similar design, can be seen at the Louvre in Paris. It is probably not a religious object, but a Standing Cup, or a Salt.

Recent research attributes these items to a silversmith whose mark was TvL or LvT. This may be Dierick Lookermans. He was a Dutch goldsmith and jeweller who worked in London for sometime and appears to have been there between 1609-12. [16]

Given the history of Tong, it is remarkable that it survived the ravages of the Civil War, and the greed of the Durants. Someone must have kept an eye on it. It is not unknown, in Shropshire and elsewhere, for Churchwardens to keep valuable church plate in their homes. For many years the Cup was housed in a special safe in the Vestry. This safe, installed in the late nineteenth century, has an outer door. Inside that is an inner door, covered with glass and bars, with its own key. It had a device in it so that if you put a coin into a slot on the door the outer door would open, and you could view the cup.

There is a crack in the crystal. This was caused by the Vicar of Donnington, who dropped it on the floor, when he was shown it by his fellow incumbent. The same notebook, which describes that incident, also records that, following a family baptism from Weston Park, the Earl of Bradford asked to borrow the Cup, in order to show it to his friends and relatives. The notebook continues *"Thirty years later the Vicar of Tong went up to Weston Park with his son to demand it back"*. This may explain the need for a complex safe.

There were always some who saw the Cup as a potential source of income for the Church. This came to a head in 1911 when plans were made for its sale. There was local uproar. A farm labourer, in Tong, wrote a letter to **The Wolverhampton Express and Star:**

"Dear Sir,

If you will send a reporter to Tong you will get some startling news for you're paper, for they have had a meeting to sell the Communion Cup belonging to Tong Church. It is 500 years old, they tried the game 16 years ago but it was stopped. We working men daren't speak. Don't show this letter to anybody or they will guess who wrote it. Farm Labourer." [17]

An earlier application had been made by the Vestry to sell the Cup in 1896. It was recorded that:

"As an offer of not less that £1,000 has been made for the gilt and crystal ciborium and provided that the proposal to sell the same meets with the approval of the Bishop, Lord Bradford, and the Chancellor of the Diocese, and that the fund so realised shall be invested to increase the Stipend of the Vicar of Tong".

The date is significant. It was the year that the Revd J. E. Auden became the Vicar. No faculty was granted then.

In 1912 a faculty was applied for in the proper manner, but the unanimous resolution of the Vestry was different

"that the proceeds of sale shall be divided in the following proportions 3/5 to increase the stipend of the Vicar of Tong (now only £115 per ann net) and 2/5 to help the funds of the Church and the expenses of the services"

This time, a full Consistory Court hearing took place on 25th February 1913. However, the Vicar and Churchwardens were faced with opposition from other parishioners, and inhabitants of the village. The application was refused.

Soon afterwards, this was the major topic of the Archdeacon of Salop's Visitation Charge. We see the Archdeacon trying to pour oil on troubled waters:

"The Archdeaconry, towards the end of last year, awakened to find itself famous as the possessor of a rare Church cup, the property of the parish of Tong. Antiquarians had long known of the existence of this cup, and that the period of its manufacture was probably toward the end of Elizabeth's reign or the beginning of the reign of James I...

I look on this proposal for its sale as a 20th century test case, not without interest to such parishes as have their own unique treasures, as of these there are not a few in Salop, the property of the Church...

...the application for a faculty for the sale of this particular cup was done in due order. The application had received the approval of the Bishop of the diocese, the patron of the living, the Vicar of the parish and that of the parishioners. It is common knowledge that in the past, in somewhat similar circumstances, no such assents were considered necessary, and historically interesting objects of value disappeared from our churches without contemporary criticism.

In the case I am referring to the faculty asked for was not granted. The chancellor based his refusal of the application, and I think rightly, on the fact that the cup has been used in the service of God and the church and that if was repulsive that an article of that kind should be alienated to a chance purchaser.

In the second place the story of the cup provides a moral. It opens up the general question of the right of the church to do what it will with its own. The President of the Society of Antiquaries in a letter to The Times expressed the opinion that if the application of Tong if granted, was certain to be followed by others, with perhaps equal or even stronger arguments to support their case."

He ended by hoping that there would be very few such applications in the future. He warned that the government might pass a bill preventing it. He ended:

"I have much sympathy with the Parish of Tong. It was quite justified in taking the action it did and very nearly brought its proposals to a successful issue. Our sympathy may also be extended to the Vicar of the parish who has for so many years devoted himself to the spiritual welfare of his parishioners, practically as his own charges." [18]

Then he adds a strange sentence:

"The Vicar can preach the Gospel but he cannot live by it".

The implication of this story is that, during the time that he had been the Vicar, Auden wanted a higher stipend. Following the court case, John Auden left the parish. It is likely that he had alienated his parishioners. Sometime later, the Cup was exhibited at a National Church Congress.

This fact might explain why in 1927, Sir Chares Mander, as Churchwarden, raised the possibility of sale again. A rich Lancastrian wished to buy it, for the new Liverpool Cathedral. The matter was not pursued any further. [19] So the Cup remains in the possession of the Parish, though it is now kept in the Treasury of Lichfield Cathedral. [20]

NOTES

[1] Quoted in Auden Vol 1 p81

[2] E. Burritt **Walks in the Black Country**

[3] This Board is still in the Church.

[4] He also donated money for "the new sepulchre at Tong". Auden Vol 1 p83.

[5] Quoted by Auden Vol 1 p31

[6] See 4 above

[7] For an up to date assessment of Bray see D. O'Connor **Three Centuries of Mission**

[8] See J. Lee **Shropshire Parochial Libraries**

[9] Beriah Botfeld **The Tong Minister's Library 1860**

[10] I found this in an old parish chest. It is now in the Shropshire Archives.

[11] See Chapter 2.

[12] The Parish of Hodnet refused to deposit its Library. Unfortunately the Archdeacons forgot to apply for the requisite faculty and this was only regularised in 1988. Thus the books are still legally the property of the Parish. The matter is regulated by the Parochial Libraries Act of 1708.

[13] Churchwarden's Accounts. 1630

[14] Griffiths pp97-8

[15] Pevsner **Shropshire** and Griffiths pp82-3

[16] See Glanville **Silver in Tudor and Early Stuart England** pp96-98, 159,166,318,405-406.

[17] **Treasure at Tong** Wolverhampton Express and Star 1911

[18] Archdeacon of Salop's Charge for 1912 (i.e. delivered in 1913).

[19] I am grateful to Mithra Tonking for investigating the Consistory Court papers.

[20] There is a fine picture of the Cup in the Reader's Digest **Treasures of Britain**.

Chapter 9
Of Clerics and Clerks

Eamon Duffy, in **The Voices of Morebath** [1], describes the life of a small village in Devon at the time of the Reformation. He does it through the eyes of the incumbent, who stayed there for fifty years. The parish accounts, written by the Vicar, give a profound insight to the Parish during great change. The story of the clergy at Tong is somewhat different. The power of the Lord of the Manor was very great, and the existence of the College of clergy meant that the ministry of the Church was more corporate. After the Reformation, Tong had only one Vicar, who stayed a very long time. That was Lewis Peitier (1688-1745). On the whole, country people have looked on the clergy with slight suspicion, realising that they would not stay for too long. The clergy were simply *"ships that pass in the night"*. A much more mobile population has changed that. Today clergy are likely to stay as long as many of the parishioners. There is a list of clergy in Appendix E.

When the College was dissolved, the lay rector was required to appoint a perpetual curate (which meant he could not be removed at the will of the patron). There is no record of the early post-Reformation clergy. The first name we have is 80 years later. He was George Meeson, curate from 1602. He is described as *"no preacher, no degree"*. He was buried, in the churchyard, in 1641. In his old age, Meeson had the help of William Southall, who was a local person, from Beamish Hall, Albrighton. Southall then became incumbent, and may have been ejected in 1643 for refusing the Cromwellian covenant. In 1646, he was Vicar of Pattingham.

Robert Hilton was Vicar of Lapley in 1638, but he was ejected from there in 1647. William Pierrepoint appointed him to Tong in 1650. This was an act of kindness in those troubled times. Hilton ran a school at Tong. His successor at Lapley (who was removed in 1660) complained that *"he did not get his arrears from 1647-9"*. (This relates to glebe income, or fees). He also complained that he had an order to pay Mrs Hilton, (even though her husband was Vicar of Tong) and that it was unfair that Hilton also held the Sutton (Stretton) Chapelry, in Staffordshire. In 1660 Hilton was re-instated at Lapley. These events demonstrate the way some clergy tried to survive, during the Commonwealth period. Many depended on kind patrons to help them out.

The next three incumbents are only known by their name. Then came Lewis Petier who was in post for 50 years. Born in Geneva, he was a considerable scholar. Not many clergy would be able to give 77 books to the Library. [2] The books reveal that he was conversant in Latin, Greek, French and Italian. Peitier was the first occupant of the new Vicarage which the Duke of Kingston had built in preparation for the sale of Tong. Thomas Hill was Peitier's curate. He was then incumbent, for three years. An incumbent called William Brown followed Hill. [3] He was there between 1748 and 1765, and would have witnessed the purchase of Tong, by George Durant (I).

The next incumbent Scrope Beardmore was an Oxford D.D. but, (like his namesake the bankrupt dandy Scrope Beardmore Davies), was an absentee. [4] In fact, between 1765 and 1843, all the incumbents were absentees and the Vicarage was rented out.

Theophilus Buckeridge was George Durant (I)'s cousin, and was Vicar of Edingale (Staffs) from 1748- 91. In Beardmore's absence, he helped out at Tong from 1765-69. Then he succeeded him. Buckeridge was a pluralist, because he was also master of St John's Hospital, which was a very lucrative post. His son, Charles Buckeridge (an Oxford D.D.) was his father's curate at Tong (1781-91). He became Rector of Newport (Shropshire) in 1790, and Vicar of Tong in 1791. He left Tong to become a Residentiary Canon of Lichfield in 1807, but he retained Newport until 1827. Later, he became Archdeacon of Coventry. After his first wife died, he married Elizabeth Slaney from Shifnal. It was probably at his suggestion, that John Mucklestone succeeded him at Tong. Mucklestone was lecturer in Divinity at Lichfield Cathedral (1807-39). He combined this work with Tong from 1807-39. He also held a living in Cheshire. Thus we see a group of clergy, who were making a considerable income, by holding a plurality of posts. This was very common at the time, and led to a popular demand to stop clergy holding several livings. In 1827 of the 10,533 benefices in England only 4,413 had resident clergy. The Pluralities Act of 1838 limited the number of livings a clergyman could hold to two. [5]

George Durant (II)'s illegitimate son, Leonard Henry St George was ordained in 1838. He helped out at Tong, before becoming incumbent in 1839. He spent two of his four years living in Normandy. After a time, George Durant feared that Leonard, with his brothers, was siding against him. So Durant told Leonard's landlord at Tong Norton to give him notice. George Durant did not attend Church; for fear that his son would "lecture him". The Vicarage was let to a family called Crockett. Leonard left Tong in 1843. He was an army chaplain from 1855-75 and spent some time in India. From 1841, there was a curate called James Issacson.

George Harding (Vicar 1843-55) was 26, when he came to Tong. He presided over the end of the Durant era. He came to Tong, after a curacy at Broughton (Staffs). Afterwards, he moved to be Rector of Cheswardine (Shropshire). He was married with three children. At Tong, they employed a nurse; a cook; a page; a housemaid; and a gardener, who was also the groom. This implies that Harding must have had some private means. He was succeeded at Tong by his brother, John Harding (1855-70). He came from Essex. Later, he was Rector of Chilton in Suffolk, and, finally, succeeded his brother, at Cheswardine.

By this time the High Church Oxford Movement calling for a deeper and more professional clergy was getting a grip on the Church of England. Tong seems to have been caught up in this. There was one curate, called John Marshall, who only stayed a year. In his final sermon he stated:

"I leave the heathen of Tong as I found them, unconverted and unconvertible."

Subsequently, he became a Roman Catholic, and taught classics at Birmingham Oratory, where he would have known Cardinal Newman. The High Church movement in Shropshire led to the establishment of an embryonic Religious Community at Stoke-on-Tern. A leading High Churchman at that time, was the Revd G. W. Woodhouse, then Vicar of Albrighton. He was a close friend of the Revd Richard Twigg, the Vicar of St James Wednesbury, who was the pioneer of Anglo-Catholic parish missions. [6] Two Woodhouse sons were both curates of Tong in John Harding's time as was Henry Francis John Jones, son of John Jones of Ruckley Grange. He also became a Roman Catholic. John Harding seems to have resided elsewhere. In 1861, George Woodhouse, the curate, was living in the Vicarage with his wife, one child and two servants.

One effect of Tractarianism, and the development of the ministry as a profession was the establishment of theological colleges. [7] Previously graduate clergy had no training, but learnt on the job. The first man at Tong to have had Theological College training was Richard Lawrence. He had been educated at Cambridge and Wells Theological College. He served four curacies at Chinnock, Westbury-on-Trym, Welshpool, and Edgmond before becoming Vicar of Tong in 1870. He was not living in the Vicarage in 1871 but stayed until 1876, when he retired to Caernarvonshire. He left a notebook on the history of Tong, which has been quoted by various subsequent writers on Tong, but it is not very accurate.

The next group of clergy were clearly able, of good education, and well off. Charles Wilson was the son of the Boden Professor of Sanscrit at Oxford. Ordained in 1840, he was Chaplain in Bombay from 1855-74. On his return, he had two short curacies in Shropshire before coming to Tong. He did not live in the Vicarage, which was occupied by Major Terrot, whose son later became Vicar of Waters Upton. In 1882 Wilson retired to Florence.

George Rivett-Carnac was educated at Harrow School, Cambridge, and Chichester Theological College. He was a considerable sportsman. He played ice hockey, and cricket. On one occasion in 1875, playing for Priory Park against the South of England, he bowled out W. G. Grace for 0, and his brother G. F. Grace for 2 in the same over. He served curacies in Norfolk and Kew, and was at Tong for eight years (1882-90). He had two subsequent livings. He inherited a Baronetcy in 1898, and died in 1932. He was married to the granddaughter of the rural poet, George Crabbe.

John Henry Courtney Clarke was an Army officer, retiring with pay as a major in 1886. The he attended Lichfield Theological College. He came to Tong, aged 43, after a curacy at Lapley. He had a family of 6 children. At the Vicarage, he employed a nurse, a cook and a parlour maid. He supervised the restoration of Tong Church. He became Rector of Tamworth in 1896, and died in 1928.

John E. Auden was one of three bothers, whose father was Rector of Horninglow in Staffordshire. One brother was also a Shropshire incumbent, and an authority on Local History. His uncle, a doctor in Birmingham, was the father of the poet W. H. Auden. [8] John Auden was born, in 1861, at Silverdale (Staffs) where his father was then the Vicar. He was educated at Shrewsbury School, and Lincoln College Oxford. He served three curacies at Carisbrooke, Wooburn, and Lichfield before becoming Vicar of Shrawardine near Shrewsbury. He came to Tong in 1896. He lived at the Vicarage with his wife, three children, and his sister. They had a cook, a housemaid, and a governess. This may imply that the children were educated at home. As already noted, he encouraged the application to sell the Tong Cup in order to increase the income of the benefice (at that time £115p.a). He left in 1913, and went to Australia. He became an Army Chaplain in 1915. In 1920 he was appointed Master of St John's Hospital, Lichfield. He retired, aged 64, in 1925, and lived in Stafford for another 20 years. Two of his daughters lived in Albrighton until they died, in the 1970s. Fascinated by local history, he contributed many papers to the Shropshire Archaeological Society. This book could not have been written without his painstaking notes. They are written in a fine, but legible hand. He sustained his interest in Tong well after he left. He battled hard to refute many false stories, which he discovered permeating community (see Chapter 13). He edited part of the Register of Shrewsbury School, was the author of the *History of the Albrighton Hunt* and the *Guide to Shropshire*.

The Revd W. Milligan was Incumbent during the First World War. Educated at Cambridge, he was ordained in the Diocese of Lichfield in 1882. He came to Tong from St Luke's Wolverhampton, in 1913.

Between the two World Wars, there were three incumbents. F. Heaton and Arthur Guiness exchanged livings. Heaton was rather aristocratic but held socialist views. He came to Tong after three curacies in London. In 1926, he became Vicar of Tenterten in Kent and Arthur Guinness moved from there to Tong. One must assume that these two men knew each other, and found the exchange mutually convenient. Around this time the patronage was transferred from the Earl of Bradford to the Bishop of Lichfield. It could be that the Earl objected to the exchange of livings; over which he had no control. Walter Grove, who came in 1935, was older than his two predecessors. He had worked in New Zealand and in the Diocese of Coventry. He left when he was 68.

W. W. Holdgate was incumbent during the Second World War. He was primarily a schoolmaster, who taught at Trent College. Then, he became successively, Headmaster of Magdalene College School, Brackley (1899-1910), and of Sutton Valence School (1910-32). He came to Tong from a living in the Diocese of Derby, at the age of 65. He wore a mortarboard and was very short, as well as being was rather lame. He was much more Low Church than his predecessors. He is remembered for being in charge of issuing gas masks. Billy Bridgewater, at the Wheelwright's shop at Tong Norton, made a fall stool for him to sit on in the pulpit. It is now used as a flower stand.

E. J. Gargery made quite an impact on Tong. Having served in the Army in the First World War, he went to Keble College Oxford in 1919. Then he went to Lichfield Theological College (where he would have been taught by his successor at Tong). He was ordained in 1922, and married the same year. After curacies in Wolverhampton and Cheam, he moved to Norfolk. From his curacies onwards, he exercised part of his ministry by producing nativity plays and other dramas. After he come to Tong, he wrote and produced the pageant *The Spirit of Tong* (see Chapter 11). His daughter, Veronica, died and as a result, he moved to Ivinghoe (Bucks) in 1954. He retired in 1962. His ashes are buried, in his daughter's grave, at Tong. He claimed to be of the same family from which Dickens took the name of the blacksmith in *Great Expectations*. Apart from his own children, he had no relations.

J. C. West was an academic, with a first class degree in Theology. Ordained in 1914, he served a curacy in Sunderland and taught at Lichfield Theological College, starting in 1919. He was 66, when he came to Tong and only stayed for 2 years. It was clear that by now the Diocese was wondering what to do with the Parish.

Brian Skelding was much younger than his three predecessors, but he only stayed a short time. He came to Tong, having served two curacies in Lichfield Diocese. It was in his time that Mr Dyer produced a simple guide to Tong Church, based on George Griffiths' earlier guide. He was interested in history, but made the great mistake of repainting Sir Henry Vernon's tomb in a manner that has greatly distressed the conservationists. When he was 38, he moved to the Liverpool Diocese. He later had two other livings in Lichfield, before retiring in 1984. He died on 1st January 2005.

Between 1950 and 1960, the population of Tong halved. The next incumbent, Albert Yates was a late ordinand and came to Tong from Palfrey in Walsall, at the age of 58. During his time, the Vicarage was sold and a new one built in the field opposite. While the building was in progress, Mr Yates lived in a flat at Donnington Rectory.

In some ways, building the new Vicarage was rather odd, because in the future the Parish could not justify a full time priest. The next incumbent, John Spencer was a senior Diocesan clergyman and a Prebendary of Lichfield Cathedral. He had spent the whole of his life in the Diocese, but he was 67 when he came to Tong, and died three years later. His widow presented communion silver in his memory.

The living was then merged with the Parish of Blymhill and Henry Horatio Follis, Vicar of Blymhill, put in charge. He was another senior priest and a fine musician. He had been Priest Vicar of Lichfield Cathedral and held the major livings of Little Aston, St. Mary's Shrewsbury and Broadway (in the Diocese of Worcester). He was a strong supporter of the British Israelite Movement.

The Archdeacon Incumbents of Tong photograph by J Whitehead

This merger clearly did not work, and it was decided to appoint someone with a Diocesan post to Tong. The first was Graham Johnson the Diocesan Youth officer. Two years later, Robert Jeffery came, from Oxford, to be Diocesan Missioner. 18 months later, he became Archdeacon of Salop. He saw no reason to move, with the result that his two successors as Archdeacon, George Frost, and John Hall, have lived at Tong. All the time the population has slowly diminished. Thus we see how the clergy at Tong have reflected ecclesiastical trends and fashions: but since the end of absentee vicars, the parishioners have been well served.

PARISH CLERKS

The Parish Clerks may have been more influential than the clergy, with the ordinary people in the Parish. They were totally part of the community, and fulfilled their tasks, alongside having other local employment. They often acted as Sexton (digging the graves), and Verger (for the services). There seems to have been a Parish Clerk all the time between 1655 and 1976.

From 1750 to 1807, the members of the Ore family held the post. Some of them were clockmakers. They lived mainly at Tong Norton and the Knowle. The family was still there in 1901. A little later, William Woolley was Parish Clerk. He was also a clockmaker, and lived at Tong Hill. Woolley was dismissed from his post, after a visiting preacher complained that there was no mirror in the vestry. Woolley called him *"a confounded cockscomb"*. George Durant (II) subsequently provided a mirror. A later parish Clerk was Andrew Cousins; he combined the post with being the village schoolmaster.

(Some identified him as the Schoolmaster in *"The Old Curiosity Shop".*)
He is buried in the Churchyard.

The Boden family held the post from 1871-1939. John Boden ran the
Post Office, and was a shoemaker. His memorial Plaque, in the Church,
reveals him as a much-respected person; but he was not educated enough to
become the Schoolteacher (a post he applied for and had been held by his
recent predecessors). His son, George, followed the same career as his
father. He was a leading bowler in the Village Cricket Team. He found the
post of Parish Clerk a useful source of additional income (see Chapter 13).
Boden made enough money to buy a house in Albrighton, and died in 1943,
aged 86. The last Parish Clerk was Harry Tindall. He was a smallholder at
Tong Hall. He had been born at Convent Lodge, when his father was Head
Gardener at the Castle. His knowledge of the Church and Churchyard was
immense, but none of it was written down. He knew where everyone was
buried. He died in 1976, aged 80, and is buried in the Churchyard. His
daughter, Joan Davies, lived with him at Tong Hall with her husband, who
also died in 1976. She moved into the Almshouses, and died in 1990.

It is noticeable that while most of the clergy moved on, the Parish
Clerks, in the main, held the post until they died. This meant that they
provided much more continuity than the clergy. The interactions, between
the Clergy and Parish Clerks, offer another insight into village life.

NOTES

[1] E. Duffy *The Voices of Morebath*
[2] For the effect of printing and books at the time see W. Gibson *The Church of England 1688-1832* pp159-166. He points out that a bookseller at Heathfield, who was the son of the Vicar, left the parish 200 books in 1736. This shows that Petier's gift was very considerable.
[3] His license is in the Diocesan archives there is no record elsewhere.
[4] V. Murray *High Society in The Regency Period* p42 Davies, being in debt, fled to Paris.
[5] O. Chadwick *The Victorian Church* Vol 1 Chapter 2
[6] John Kent *Holding the Fort* p255
[7] Anthony Russell *The Clerical Profession*
[8] See the autobiography by Humphrey Carpenter

Part Three: Village Life

Chapter 10
Living in Tong - the story of the Houses

George Griffiths provided the text of a document of 1719. It defined the boundaries of Parish and Manor of Tong, as it was used at the Rogationtide beating of the bounds. The parish boundary remains the same today. On the 19th and 20th May 1718, the beating of bounds took two days to complete. The parishes of Donnington, Brewood, and Weston under Lizard, Sherriffhales and Shifnal surround it. [1] But there is another way to envisage the Parish. This emerges very clearly from the Census figures. Tong was a private domain with the Castle at its centre. Some sort of Toll House guarded each of the roads into Tong. Burlington was a Toll House; Convent Lodge was the entrance near Kilsall, and there were similar cottages at Ruckley and Bishops Wood.

Not only was it a private domain, but also an entirely self-contained one, with a self-sustaining community. The College, and subsequent Schools, offered education. Care of the elderly was in the hands of the College and then the Almshouses. The Castle and the Church were the focal points for social cohesion, and controlled the work people did. Agriculture required supporting tradesmen, like carpenters, blacksmiths, bakers, shoemakers: and the necessary alehouses, of which Tong had its fair share. The development of Tong Forge, and Clock-making gave some industrial diversity to the employment pattern. The tenants had to supply the Castle with coal. There were domestic servants, employed at the Castle, and in other private houses, like the Vicarage.

But there were other layers of community life. There were those whose social standing depended on their paid work. Into this category would come the Vicar, the Doctor, the Parish Nurse or Midwife, the Undertaker (usually the Carpenter), the Schoolmaster and the Policeman. Another figure, usually hovering in the background, was the landowner's Agent, upon whom many would have depended for their employment. There were families of reasonable means, who were not so dependent on the feudal pattern. These became Churchwardens, Church Treasurers, members of the Parish Council and they were an essential part of the whole fabric of the village.

↑ A5

Old Bush House

Offoxey Road

Bell Inn

Norton Farm

Tong

Shaw Lane

Norton

Castle Hill

Friars Lane

A41

Tong Hill Farm

Hubbal Lane

Church Farm

B / W Cottages

Parish Hall

Old School

Old School House

Tong Priory

Shifnal 2 miles

Quarry

Holytree Cottage

Old Post Office

The Red House

Almshouses

Vicarage

Tong Church

Tong College (site of)

Tong House

Tong Hall

Police House

Church Pool

Telford

Tong

N

Tong Castle (site of)

M54

Tong Park Farm

Neachley Hall

Convent Lodge

New Buildings Farm

M6

1 Km

Cosford

Map of Tong Village

(see page 10 for map of the whole parish)

Auden, in his Notes [2], describes many of the houses in Tong, and the people who lived in them. Each house tells part of the story of the village. To gain a picture of village life, we will summarise some of these stories. Richard Gough, in his seventeenth century *"History of Myddle"* [3], began his account of village life by listing where everyone sat in church. Then he described what the people did. Here we are trying to tell the village history through the houses.

NEW BUILDINGS FARM is on the Cosford side of the M54 motorway. This tall red brick building has an enclosed yard. The origins of the first house here are not known but it may have been called "Hollis Field Farm". This was the home of Robert Burd, one of those who had helped King Charles escape in 1651. In 1670, he was granted a Royal annuity of £30 p.a. for his help in this matter. Burd was the Innkeeper of the Talbot Inn at Albrighton. He retired to the farm in 1664. He was Churchwarden of Tong in 1666. [4] A descendant, who had gone to Canada, was still trying to claim this annuity in 1938, but the case seems to have been lost owing to the Second World War. [5] The present house was built by George Durant (II), sometime before 1809. The Revd B. Ward stated that he was born there in 1791 and was the third of 6 sons. Later, his father moved to Tong Park Farm. [6]

George Durant wanted to ruin the view for Mr Bishton. He had a major feud with Mr Bishton, over the building of a new pool; and because Bishton helped out his son, George (III), when he fell out with his father. The farm, incorporating a Malthouse (still in use until the 1980s), was only ever a small farm and had 9 acres in 1851.

KILSALL HALL lies across the A41 near the road to Neachley just outside the parish. Previously there had been a house called *"Kilsall Red House"* in the field in front of the present Kilsall Hall. It was then known as *"Kilsall White House"*. Bishton lived in the Red House, but after the building of the farm, it was demolished, and he moved to a new House at Neach Hill. [7] The Bishtons owned Kilsall for over 300 years. In the second half of the nineteenth century, Kilsall Hall was rented by George Thompson Hartley, son of John Hartley (who rented Tong Castle). In 1917, Kilsall was rented by the head of Manders Paint Works, Charles Mander (1884-1951), from another paint manufacturer, Daniel Jones. His wife described their first visit:

"See over Kilsall Hall. Tong. Horrid day. Most charming place, so much white panelling, large drawing room, square smoke room, square panelled hall, oblong dining room and quaint wee room off hall; three stair-cases… So cold inside seemed quite warm when we came out again; wanted a lot of work doing to it." [8]

Mander's brother did some research, revealing that the place, known as 'Cylle's hall,' was first mentioned in 1006. There was a farmhouse there in 1593.

Sir Charles Mander had a distinguished career in the Army in the First World War. He fought in Egypt and Palestine. He was the third member of the Mander family to be Mayor of Wolverhampton. He was also Lord Lt of Staffordshire, and Master of the Albrighton Hunt. As a Churchman, he was a major figure and fundraiser in the Diocese of Lichfield, and Churchwarden of Tong. In 1951, he died of a cerebral haemorrhage, at the age of 66, while chairing 'an acrimonious meeting' of the Albrighton Hunt. His memorial in Tong Church has the inscription *"Many waters cannot quench love"*.

The next owners of Kilsall were the Hibbert-Hingstons, who lived there for nearly 40 years. Andrew Hibbert-Hingston was for many years Churchwarden, following in the Mander tradition.

CONVENT LODGE is near the new roundabout. It was built at the main entrance to Tong Castle. The elaborate gates erected there were moved to Wolverhampton, and are now at the Ironbridge Museum. We have already notes that George Durant (II) required the gatekeeper to be dressed as a Nun. In 1871, a Labourer called Bowdler lived there. (See watercolour illustration in central section). In 1881 it became the home of the head gardener of the Castle. The first there was called Bevan. In 1891, Charles Tindall, who had trained at Veitches Nurseries in London, succeeded him. He was paid 21 shillings a week. After ten years he was given an extra four shillings. The Lodge was occupied until the middle 1960s (having no gas or electricity). During the excavations of Tong Castle, it was used for storing the finds. Lord Bradford then used the Lodge and surrounding land, as a centre for paint balling exercises.

TONG PARK FARM is one of the few remaining farms in the Village. It is situated just off the road into Tong. The Park was an enclosure attached to Tong Castle. The present farmhouse was originally the lodge for the Deer Park. A plaque on the building states that the Duke of Kingston refurbished in 1736. It has remained a farmhouse ever since. The building was destroyed by fire in 1849, while the village was celebrating the coming of age of George Durant (IV). It was rebuilt the following year. It now has an extension, which incorporates a roof beam from Hubbal Grange (see below). In 1861, the farm was 340 acres and employed four men, and four boys. In 1944 a V1 bomb was dropped in a wood on the farm and another at Tong Hill Farm.

TONG HALL. In the Village, just past the 1970s Police House is Tong Hall. George Durant (II) built this rather unattractive building, in 1842. He left it to his second wife, Celeste, to be held in trust for his son, Augustine St Alban Durant. Celeste did not live there for very long. On the front is a tablet inscribed *"AUG St. A D 1837"*. This is not the date of the house, but the year of Augustine's birth. On the back, a tablet reads *"TONG HALL 1842"*. On the south side, there used to be two niches containing statues of St Augustine and St Alban. The house was sold with some land to the Bradford Estate in 1867. It became a small farm. In 1881, it had 37 acres, and was run by a family called Milner. The son was a maltster, and he succeeded his father in 1901. Later the Tindalls moved there. Harry Tindall ran the smallholding. He was also Church Sexton and Parish Clerk. His daughter Joan Davies moved from there to the Almshouses in 1976, when her husband died. She and her father had a vast knowledge of Tong.

THE VICARAGE. Next to Tong Hall is the old Archery Field. It subsequently, became part of the Incumbent's Glebe. A new Vicarage was built there in 1962. Since 1980, it has been the residence of the Archdeacon of Salop, and it was enlarged to provide office space for the Archdeacon. Behind it is another house built by Mr Ingram Brown. He moved into it, when he handed over Tong Park Farm to his son.

TONG HOUSE. Opposite the new Vicarage is the old one, which was sold in 1961. This redbrick Vicarage was built by the Duke of Kingston in 1725. Before then, the clergy had either lived in the College, or the Castle. The Duke built it, as part of the process of disposing of Tong Castle. The house had four rooms on the first two floors, some of them panelled. It included one room to house the Tong Minister's Library. A top floor, not visible from the front, has three large rooms, and a boxroom, designed for the servants. It had a stable, hayloft and brewhouse. The Parish Terrier of 1789 states that the Vicarage had a pigsty, coalhouse, a courtyard and an orchard. The Terrier also states: *"The two pews on the north side of the pulpit and* *reading desk belong to the Vicar"*. George Durant (II) took the orchard land to provide a new entrance to the Castle. The Earl of Bradford paid for the restoration of the Vicarage in 1873.

THE ALMSHOUSES. This single story, redbrick building, next to the Vicarage, contains four almshouses, run by local trustees, for elderly members of the community. George Durant (II) built these almshouses in 1804 replacing the College Hospice. In 1763, Mr. Coles reported that the occupants were provided with 40 shillings, and a shift and gown each year. [9] The present building, originally, had eight small units, but they were altered to four in the 1960s. In 1861, all eight were in use, including two housing a mother and child. So the age range was from 80 to 10. In 1871, only six were occupied. In 1891, there was a 19-year-old girl old, appointed to look after the residents. When Tong Castle was sold, one of the conditions of the sale was that the owner paid £34 p.a. for the maintenance of the almshouses. The same sum is paid today.

THE RED HOUSE. This tall, distinguished house dominates the centre of the Village. It was called the Red House, because it was the only house not white washed. In 1739, it belonged to the Duncalfes. The parish map shows that they had several other plots of land. This was a Cheshire family, of some distinction and seemed to have moved to Tong around 1630. Another tenant was Thomas Clews, who was a maltster and seeds man. He was Churchwarden of Tong between 1822 and 1824. The Duncalfes sold the house to George Durant (II) in 1832. During the years 1834-44, it was *"The Malt Shovel Inn"*. In the 1930s a Mrs Hastings lived there, whose son is commemorated on the Second World War memorial in the Church. As with Kilsall Hall, the occupants of The Red House (like the Wests and the Tucks) have often played a major role in the Church and Village.

THE OLD POST OFFICE is next to the Red House. It was originally crenellated, and was built as the East Lodge to Tong Castle. For many years it was the Village Shop. Dorothy Ore was one shopkeeper. She was well known as an herbalist, and provided many natural cures. George Durant (II) had a notice outside with the words *"NO TRUST"* (that would mean no credit), someone added underneath *"NO TRADE"*.

Watercolour of the East Lodge from George Durant (II)'s notebook

Later John Boden, who combined being a postmaster and shoemaker, with being Parish Clerk, ran the Post Office. The Bodens were a large family, and at one time three generations were living there. George Boden succeeded his father in all these functions. He married Miss Williams, a teacher at the School. Later, she opened a private school in Albrighton [10]. The property was owned by Lord Bradford, but purchased from him by Syd Green whose mother was the last postmistress. Syd died in 1987.

HOLLY TREE COTTAGE, next door, was the home of village policeman for many years.

THE CHURCH FARM is a black and white house, opposite the Church. This was the old Coaching Inn (The Bell Inn). It has some fine seventeenth century panelled rooms. George Durant (II) moved the Inn further up the road. He thought it unseemly to be so near the Church. The house is reported to be haunted by a horse. It had been a farm, but for many years has been a Riding School, run by Mrs Joan Bates. Her son, Simon, the well-known disc jockey, was brought up here. He played a part in Parish Youth Club activities. Many people have become familiar with Tong through attending the Riding School.

<u>Church Farm</u>

Going up the Tong Hill, from there, are some refurbished black and white houses. William Woolley who was another clockmaker occupied one until the 1850s.

Next comes **THE VILLAGE HALL** where many events take place, and is used as the Village Polling Station. A wooden building, erected in 1910, it has been modernised in recent years.

THE OLD SCHOOL (formerly called TONG COURT) is the former School, was built in 1872. [11] This was turned into a spacious house and lived in for the next 20 years by Mr and Mrs Stallard. Jim Stallard was Churchwarden.

Next door is **THE OLD SCHOOL HOUSE** built for the Schoolteacher, at the same time as the School. The first teacher to live there was John Longstaff.

Beyond this house, is the old Tong Quarry, which provided sandstone for many of the Tong buildings. Over the years, it has been filled up with garden rubbish. The Hill gets very steep, at this point.

At the top of the Hill, on the left, is **THE PRIORY**. The original house was built by George Durant (II) and replaced in the early 1960s. It has stables, and was always one of the gentry houses in Tong. In 1841, a 56-year-old lady called Sarah Brown occupied it. From 1861-81, a family called Fisher lived there. Mr Fisher was a London barrister. By 1891, it was occupied by Mrs Wilkinson and her daughter. Colonel Ashworth lived there from 1930-40. The next occupants were the Ridgewells. When they left, a new house was built, Next to the Priory was a reservoir that had water pumped up into it. Until the arrival of mains water, this provided all the water for the Village.

Further along, there used to be black and white cottages: one of which was described as *"Little Nell's Cottage"*. These have been replaced by farm labourer's houses for **TONG HILL FARM**. This has been a farm, since at least 1739. At one time, it was owned by the Parker family. They were local weavers. In 1861, it had 160 acres and 4 labourers. From 1841 into the twentieth century, there was a family called Bennion. Then they moved to Tong Norton. The Morris family have been there, ever since.

Much further along Hubbal Lane, is **HUBBAL GRANGE**. This is one of Tong's historic sites. It is now a ruin. It was originally the Grange Farm of Black Ladies Convent. At the Dissolution, it became the property of the Giffards of Chillington. In the seventeenth century, it was leased to the Penderell family. There were five Penderell brothers, who like the Giffards, were recusant Roman Catholics. William Penderell was the under steward of the Chillington estate. After the battle of Worcester Charles fled to Whiteladies, where, with Richard Penderell, they planned a failed escape, via Madeley into Wales. [12] After the Restoration, the Penderells received a Royal annuity. In order to disguise the King, William Penderell cut off his hair. He kept the hair, and sold bits, to supplement his income. George Durant (II) demolished the main part of Hubbal Grange and built a smaller house, which is now within Tong Park Farm. Even in 1933 there were stories around that Hubbal was where Charles had hidden himself. Robinson quotes a Mr Kingston:

'It is a much restored cottage standing in the midst of fields, lonely and difficult to approach... A comparatively modern oven was pointed out as being the place where Charles hid himself. We objected that a good sized man 'more than two yards high' could scarcely get into so small a space but the good wife overruled our objection declaring that 'there's no knowing what you would do if they were after you.'" [13]

Richard Salter lived there in the 19th century. In 1901 there was a family called Bowen, Mr Bowen drove steam engines. The last family there were the Hunchbacks. It was already vacant before the Second World War. The house finally collapsed in 1979.

TONG NORTON. In the Middle Ages, Tong Norton was a separate township, and includes the site of Castle Hill. It is reached from Tong Church by a road called *"Friars Lane"* (probably a Durant invention). The road continues on to Weston under Lizard. Tong Norton has as many houses as the Village of Tong. Several houses have been built since 1980. In 1739 there were three farms at Tong Norton.

The **BELL INN FARM** surrounded the Inn on the Newport Rd. Mr Page, the licensee of the Inn, was also involved in the transport business, and employed carters. In 1871, Mr Leach ran the Inn and the Farm with 90 acres. By 1891, there was a Welsh family there called Davies. They had moved to Tong from Corwen (North Wales), and they employed two Welsh labourers. At the other end of this road, was **NORTON FARM**, with **TONG NORTON FARM**. In between is the sixteenth-century house, which was occupied by the Salter family in 1631. The Salters were an old Shropshire family, who were in Oswestry in 1211. They moved to Newport, where Sir John Salter built Salter Hall, in the sixteenth century. His nephew, Thomas, moved to Wrockwardine Manor. His grandson, George Salter moved to Tong. He is buried, with his wife and daughter, in Tong Church, near the Stanley Tomb. The family moved around Tong, and at different times were at Rosary Lodge, and Lizard Grange Farm. They moved back to Tong Norton in 1913. Other members of the family are buried in Tong Churchyard. Their descendant, the Revd John Salter has traced a fascinating family history. It connects them with many Royal families in Europe, including King Alfonso VIII of Castile, King Edward I of England, Louis IX of France, and with a number of leading Shropshire families. [14]

THE OLD BUSH HOUSE was originally "The Bush Inn". Near it had been the Blacksmiths. At the corner of the road was the old Carpenter's Shop now replaced a modern house. Next, was the Wheelwright's shop, which has been modernised. Just up Offoxey Road is Shaw Lane. This contains a line of brick cottages, owned by Lord Bradford. Norton East Farm used to be at the top of the Lane. The house was burned down in 1903. In the eighteen century, the lane contained a cockpit, for Cockfighting.

<u>Watercolour of the Blacksmith's Cottages from George Durant (II)'s</u>
<u>notebook</u>

KNOLL FARM. Friars Lane continues up to Weston Park. This part of the road was improved by Lord Bradford in 1869. It had previously been a lane given accesses to the allotments, which were flooded to create Norton Mere. A little way up on the right, is Knoll Farm. It was, for many years, the home of Lord Bradford's Clerk of Works and later his Farm Manager. It is now a private house. (See watercolour illustration in central section). It is just below Knoll Hill. It was there, at the suggestion of the Earl of Beaconsfield (Disraeli), Lord Bradford erected a flag Tower in 1883. The Tower was built near the monument erected by George Durant (II). [15] Land here was incorporated into Weston Park. The result was that the 260 acres of the farm in 1851 had been reduced to 190 acres by 1871.

On the other side of the road is **NORTON MERE**, which was part of George Durant (I)'s landscaping. The lake is about three quarters of a mile long and 100 yards wide. The Mere was made by damming up the brook at the southern end. This provided the water for the Lodge Lake, near the Castle. At the end of the Mere, there is an island, containing the ruins of an old cottage. Next to it was one of the Durant pyramids, containing a privy. Over the door was the Latin Inscription *"PARVA SED APTA"* (small but convenient) and at the other end *"SOLITAR"*.

OFFOXEY ROAD. There was an old road from the Knoll to the Holt. In 1815 George Durant gained permission to divert it, so that there was a straight road from Tong Norton to Bishops Wood. [16] Along the road are a few houses and farms.

On the right is **OFFOXEY FARM** that, in 1861, had 472 acres and employed 8 men and 2 boys. It is now just a private house. Further, on the right, is a turning leading to **HOLT FARM** and **MEASEHILL FARM**. Holt is first mentioned in the Churchwarden accounts for 1671, but it may well be older. At the foot of the Knoll Tower is a plaque cast at Tong Forge and came from the Holt. It had the crest of a dove (or martlet), and a shield, dated 1613. The Holt Farm was later incorporated into Measehill. In 1718 it was called *"Morall's Meisell"*. The word *"meese"* or *"meise"* is Anglo Saxon for a winding track. This means *"The house with a winding track"*. In 1819, there was a bad fire at the farmhouse. By 1851, the farm employed ten men, and one boy. It had 165 acres but ten years later had grown to 222 acres. Ingram Brown (of Tong Park Farm) had a brother called, West Brown who farmed at Measehill. It was then taken over by his son, but now all the farmland has been incorporated into the Bradford Estate.

Further along, is **WHITE OAK FARM**. This was originally called Wood Farm. The present name came from a large Oak tree, which was whitewashed to help night-time travellers. In 1851, the farm had 186 acres and employed 8 men. In 1828 a prize-fight took place there, between F. Samson of Birmingham and *"Big Brown"* of Bridgnorth. The prize was £500, and the fight lasted for 42 rounds. The two men had fought each other before, but this time Brown fixed the fight. He ruined his backers, many of who had pawned their beds to him. The Shropshire Quarter Sessions dealt with serious offences during this fight, and commented that such events were: *"destructive of the public peace and injurious to the property and endangering the lives of individuals in the parishes of Tong and Albrighton"*.

On the corner of Offoxey Road, and Bishops Wood is another house called **WHITE OAK LODGE**. It was formerly a public house called "The Acorn" or "The Royal Oak." It was built be George Durant in 1818, and was the scene of one of his illicit affairs. (See watercolour illustration in central section). On the pigsty are carved the words *"TO PLEASE THE PIGS"* and over the Cow House *"RANDS DES VACHES"* (rows of Cows). This corner, which is the end of the Parish, also marks the Shropshire/ Staffordshire border.

We now look at the part of the Parish on the other side of the A41. Much of it was the Castle land. The old road used to go through the Village, but it was bypassed, after a child was killed on the village road. It is important to envisage the Church as situated in the grounds of the Castle.

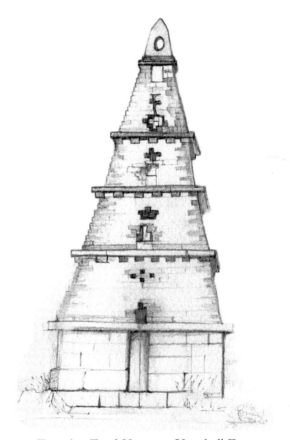

Egyptian Fowl House at Vauxhall Farm

On the road to Shifnal is **VAUXHALL FARM**. The house was a fishing cottage, on the edge of the Lodge Lake, covering some 20 acres. It contained George Durant (II)'s famous pyramid Fowl House. In 1901 the lake had diminished and it became a farm, which was rented to Albert Williams. In 1948 the water was drained off, the southern end was planted with trees, and the land tenanted to Vauxhall Farm. When it was still a

Lodge, a Roman Catholic labouring family, called Swan occupied it. Nurse Doran, who was the Durant family Nurse, also lived there. When she was dying, she kept on moaning about money. (It is probable that George Durant had not paid her.) Mrs Swan tied a crucifix to the end of the bed, and told her to think about the Lord instead. Nurse Doran was also known for her saying in Leap Years:

"Well, Good Friday will be on Saturday this year, whoever may live to see it".
With the death of Bob Owen, the last tenant, the farm was taken back into the Bradford Estate.

Further down the road is the entrance to the **RUCKLEY ESTATE**. Earlier, Ruckley Grange belonged to Buildwas Abbey and had been given to them by Philip de Belmeis (Lord of Tong 1138-9). At the Dissolution it was given to the Earl of Powys. In 1634, Ruckley Wood Farm was sold to Francis Foster, who had previously leased it. It then passed through several families including the Salters, the Jobbers and the Johnsons. Ruckley Wood was owned by the Duke of Kingston, and was sold to the Durants with the Castle. In 1818, the estate was in the ownership of M. A. Slaney who established a lake there. He sold it to Mr Bishton in 1813. John Bishton pulled the house down, and built a new one in 1820. In 1849, it was bought by George Jones of Shackerley Hall. Also, he bought the Farm at the sale of the Castle Estate. In 1851, Ruckley Wood Farm had 130 acres, and employed five men. [17] There were financial problems, and the estate was sold in 1874 to Mr Horton of Priorslee. In 1896, the owner was John Reid Walker, who rebuilt the house. Whenever he travelled to Tong by train, after it had left Cosford, he used to pull the communication cord. He then handed to the guard his fine, and walked the few yards to his house. [18]

Opposite the entrance to Ruckley is the West Lodge to the Castle. For many years it was called *"The Firs"*. The house had a large dome in the middle set on sloping grounds, and is a typical Durant construction. Nearby, was another Durant house called *"Rosary Lodge"* This was the North Lodge House, and occupied by farm labourers.

Across the road, and turning north, is **TONG FORGE**. A stream runs through this part of Tong, providing much needed water for irrigation, and industry. It was here that industrial Tong developed. In 1563 the Earl of Shrewsbury, who could not sell his trees, turned them into charcoal and developed a forge, for iron production. It produced 100 tons of iron a year. The unprocessed iron came from a furnace at Shifnal. There were two forges, both of which closed in the nineteenth century. As late as 1918, it was possible to collect quantities of iron slag. During the restoration of Tong Church a token of John Wilkinson (dated 1792) was found. He was the iron master at Tong, during the Napoleonic Wars. He controlled forges at Snedshill and Willey, and may have contracted out work to Tong. He died in 1808.

The Tong Clockmakers were established alongside the Forge. The most notable of these was John Baddeley. He was baptised in Tong Church in 1720. His father was a blacksmith. When he was 18, he decided to become a clock and watchmaker. He studied mechanics, and, in 1762, began working on optics, and he constructed a reflective telescope. Later, he moved to Albrighton, and is buried there. Shaw's *Staffordshire* comments on him:

"His superiority as a clock maker will be told for some years to come by the numerous domestic and turret clocks substantially constructed by him in every part of the country within many miles of Albrighton where he long resided." [19]

He made the clock for Tong Church. It was in use until 1984; the mechanism is on display in the Church.

North of the Forge, is **LIZARD GRANGE** and **LIZARD MILL**. There is reference to the Lizard in the twelfth century manuscript of Peterborough Monastery. [20] It relates to the Anglo-Saxon period when the Lizard was owned by Peterborough. In 1143, Philip de Belmeis granted the Arosian Canons (a religious order) all the land, between Watling Street and Neachley, for the foundation of a Church in honour of *"Holy Mary, Mother of God"*. When the canons moved further north, to Lilleshall Abbey, the Lizard became their Grange Farm. When Lilleshall Abbey was dissolved, the Lizard lands went to the Duke of Sutherland, who sold them to Lord Bradford. They were never part of the Tong Estate. It must have been near here that Charles, on his way to the battle of Worcester, encamped with his troops in 1651. The old Lizard House no longer exists, but there is still a farmhouse. Lizard Grange Farm had 149 acres and 2 labourers in 1881. Lizard Mill Farm was a mill making flour, as well as a farm with 100 acres. In 1881 there was a family called Bloxham, who were succeeded by the Watters family.

Further up the A41 is **TONG HAVANNAH** consisting of four houses. It was so named by George Durant (I) to commemorate his participation in the sack of Havannah. At the crossing with the A5 road was Pickmere Island. Here had been here a **PICK MERE** – a fishing pool, stocked with pike for the use of the College. Also, at **BURLINGTON**, on the main road, was a Toll House. It guarded the Northern entrance to Tong.

This survey reveals how every house, and their occupants, add to the story of Tong. We see here a process of change, from a strong feudal society to a much more diverse one. But the heavy hand of the Durants leaves its mark all over the place.

As startling are the great changes, which have taken place since the demise of the Castle. From a large number of farms there are now only four. At one time there were at least five Public Houses in Tong; now there is only one. At one time every trade, for a self-sustaining community, was there; now there is very little. Similarly, over the last fifty years the population has dropped dramatically and the old feudal pattern has gone.

The 2001 Census profile reveals a new pattern emerging. It is a much more affluent village. [21] The population has further diminished. It was 500 in 1950, and 250 in 1980; but, by 2001, it has reduced to 208, in spite of some new house building. There are only 26 children under 18, and over half the population (110) is over 45. But, we can also a note a tendency for the older residents to move away following retirement. There are only 100 households, a third of which have only one person. There are 19 pensioner households. The entire population is white, and only three not of British ethnic origin. Half the homes are privately owned, and half rented. Every home has central heating. Most of the employed population is in professional or managerial occupations. This is quite the reverse of a hundred years earlier. Only 12 households have no car, and half have two or more cars. But, perhaps more significantly, 17 people work from home, revealing a trend away from commuting. This may indicate, with new technology, many more may work from home in the future. So there is potential for a more self-sustaining community. Thus the Village continues to change, and the stories are still being made.

NOTES

[1] G. Griffiths *History of Tong and Boscobel* pp132-153

[2] Auden Notes Vol 1

[3] R. Gough *History of Myddle*

[4] See [2]

[5] See National Archive T164/186/1

[6] See Auden's Notes vol 1 p43

[7] D. H. Robinson *The Wandering Worfe* pp64

[8] See C. N. Mander *Varnished Leaves* pp273-333

[9] *The Gentleman's Magazine* 1763

[10] On George Boden see Chapters 9 and 13.

[11] See Chapter 11.

[12] For a historical account see R. Ollard *The Escape of Charles II after the Battle of Worcester*. See also Chapter 13

[13] See 7 above p61.

[14] John Salter was at College with me. He spent many years as Vicar of St Dunstan in the West (Fleet Street) and St Silas Pentonville. He was also chairman of the Anglican and Eastern Churches Association. He preached at a Tong School reunion in 198. Following his retirement, he became a Uniate Greek Catholic Priest in 2004. I am grateful to him for sharing his detailed knowledge of Tong.

[15] See Chapter 4

[16] See Auden Vol 1 pp79-81

[17] For a detailed account see H.F. Vaughn *History of Ruckley*

[18] See 7 above p29. There is a large Reid Walker plot in the Churchyard.

[19] Quoted in Auden Vol 1 pp36-7.

[20] See *The Anglo Saxon Chronicle* p37.

[21] 2001 Census profile for the Parish of Tong produced by SAS

Photograph of the Village of Tong (Sharkey early 1960s)

Chapter 11
Scenes from Village Life

The Tong Parish Magazine, from the turn of the nineteenth century, paints a picture of a place, which is still in a feudal and dependent mode. [1] In the 1890s, there was a clothing club, a shoe club, and a reading room. In 1896, seventy people attended a Christmas party held in the Schoolroom, and *"two babies were packed away in a clothes basket in the tea room".* Thirty people attended a party for Church workers, and the annual distribution of calico, by the Tong Charities, disposed of 480 yards. There were three football teams, a Ladies Working Party, a girls' sewing class, and a branch of the Mother's Union (finally disbanded in 1981). The Sunday School thrived, and the village school received a good inspector's report. In 1897, for Queen Victoria's Diamond Jubilee, there were sports, flags, and meals:

"Luncheon for men was provided in the Schoolroom by Mrs Bowers of Albrighton. The women and children had tea in the Post Office provided by Mr Boden. We are glad to say that the catering gave general satisfaction. The number attending were 133 men, 123 women, and 132 children."

Community life included parties, fetes, and outings. A visit from Lord Bradford was like a visit from Royalty. On the occasion of his coming of age, Lord Newport (the eldest son) visited Tong School. There was a loyal address, and a presentation of gifts. There must have been a real sense of change after the sale of the Castle, as it was followed by the new School, the refurbished Vicarage, and the Restoration of the Church. It was also a time of economic growth, in the West Midlands. The building of the Shrewsbury to Wolverhampton Railway had brought Irish workers into the area. Work became available outside the Village. Tong Castle, Ruckley Grange and Kilsall Hall, were all occupied by industrial magnates. New transport brought people out from the West Midlands, to visit the area.

Tong was proud of itself. This is made very clear in a song performed at a Parish Concert in 1911:

"In the village of Tong, I have not lived long
But I am sure you'll agree with me saying,
It's the best place on earth, and there's never a dearth
Of all things that makes life worth living.
It's a beautiful spot, and it's never too hot,

140

And it's not very often too cold;
So when there's no more of fighting and war,
I'll settle down here and grow old.

Peace, peace, here we have peace,
I'll know I can't put it too strong,
I just want to praise all the people and ways,
Of the beautiful village of Tong.

Now every year, we live in great fear
That there'll be another election
And the papers are full of how poor old John Bull
Hesitates 'twixt Free Trade and Protection.
Oh these Suffragette fights and the John Redmondites
Of which all the "Rad" party's composed.
We're sick of them all, they're not wanted at all,
Our member goes up unopposed.

Peace, Peace leave us in peace,
We think all elections are wrong,
Would we still have to vote, if we lived in a boat,
On the beautiful waters of Tong?

There's a Post Office here, and a 'pub' fairly near,
And castle that is very handsome,
But I'm sorry to say, it is crumbling away,
Though the site is worth a king's ransom,
We've a very big bell,
And six others as well,
And some very fine fellows who ring them
And the rest of Tong's joys
I will leave to you boys
Who are much better to sing them.

Peace, peace don't you want peace?
I'm sure I've been singing too long
I fear I have been the one blot on the scene
Of the Amateur Concert at Tong."

This shows the last, smug, throws of feudalism. The one thing Tong, with the rest of England, did not get was peace and in the 1914-18 war twelve men were killed in action; eight of them were aged under 26. Others will have returned from the War, deeply affected by the experience.

TONG SCHOOL

The School is a good measure of community and social change. We have seen how education began, with one of the members of Tong College responsible for teaching the children. There is an account, from 1546, of the Vicar running a school. In 1686, there is reference to a Schoolhouse, though it was not occupied at the time. It is clear from the 1725 deed of the Duke of Kingston that the schoolmaster was paid £4 p.a. for teaching ten boys. The 1779 Terrier refers to *"A schoolhouse with garden adjacent to the same for the use of the Schoolmaster"*. Lady Pierrepoint left £4 p.a. to teach poor girls to read. At this time, the schoolhouse seems to have been at the west end of the Church, near the almshouses. [2]

George Durant (I) must have demolished the school along with the College Hospice. After this, there was some teaching at Tong Norton. In 1810 the Vestry agreed that:

"The children who attend the Sunday School and the Free School shall annually be clothed at Easter, each girl to have a gown and bonnet and the boys to have a tight jacket and trousers and a cloak every two years."

George Durant (II) built a new school and the schoolmaster was paid £10 p.a. By 1819, there were 22 boys and 31 girls at the school. The Schoolmaster also ran the Sunday School, for which he was paid an extra £5 p.a. The School building was on Tong Hill and was a strange building with the village lock up underneath, and the Classroom on the top. (This was probably on the site, where the Village Hall now stands.) On the wall outside, there was a tablet reading *"Ecole des Belles Lettres"*. This was the building visited by Elihu Burritt in 1854. [3]

The School was becoming even more organised and new rules were established:

"All the scholars to be taught reading, writing and accounts and the girls knitting and sewing. School hours in winter in the morning from eight to twelve and in the evening from two till four, in the summer from seven till nine and then till twelve. In the evening from two till five. Holidays, one week at Easter, four weeks at harvest and two weeks at Christmas. Any child living in the parish or belonging to it, to be received into the school with a ticket from the minister and churchwardens, their respective ages to be lain on the vestry table once a quarter on the Sunday after the quarter day. All the scholars to be brought by the master to Church every Sunday."

These rules reflect changes in social conditions. There was a need for the children to help with the harvest. Most of the teachers seem to stay about ten years. John Longstaff (1851- 71) was an antiquarian, who wrote some detailed notes on the Church.

By 1870, the new Education Act required more to be done. So Lord Bradford offered a new site for the School, and a schoolteacher's house. The new building cost £414 9s. 8d. It was opened in April 1872, and the administration remained with the Vicar and Churchwardens. When it opened, there were 25 boys and 27 girls, but the numbers grew steadily to a total of 90. The attendance of the pupils was sporadic. But this was not all of the children in Tong. At this time, there were 250 children, aged under 19, in the Village. The first teacher, at the new school, only lasted a year. He was succeeded by James Inglis, whose teaching received a very unfavourable report from School Inspectors. He also fell out with the Vicar. Then followed a long period of stability under Thomas Greener. He was at the School from 1882 to 1924. His successor was Miss Clara Breese, who stayed until 1947. So these last two teachers, between them, covered a period of 67 years. Miss Breese was there during the Second World War. This was a time when life was very fluid, with RAF children, coming and going, from the huts in the Castle grounds. One former pupil remembers knitting socks, and collecting books, to send to the troops. The last teacher was Mrs Dyer. She stayed until the school closed in 1960.

The school logbooks give an insight into school and community life. [4] Very often the school was closed, because of fever in the area. Attendance was never more than 70% per child. The reason for this was a mixture, caused by potato picking, helping on farms, or simply playing truant. One child was expelled for an unmentionable deed. Some entries reveal the teacher's anxieties. An entry in 1893 reads: *"Harry Wedge swallowed a pin. It would be a help if teachers were told what to do on these occasions"*.

In 1929, Miss Breese did seem to know what to do: *"Janet Matthews, aged five, pushed a button up her nose which lodged there and we have to take her to Shifnal Hospital."*

The Butler Education Act of 1944 was a death knell to small village schools. Numbers of pupils, at Tong, declined to less than fifty; and the rapid growth of Albrighton meant it had two primary schools, which Tong children could attend. Mrs Dyer's final entry reads: *"July 20th 1960 My resignation takes effect today. This day Tong School closes."*

The number of children in the Village continues to decline.

GAMES PEOPLE PLAY

Mr Clarke, of Tong Norton, wrote an account of some of the tricks, which boys played on each other. [5] One was called *"Catching the Owlet"*. The idea was to ask a young farm hand to go to the blacksmith's shop, after hours. He was told that there was an owlet stuck up the chimney, and was asked to go up the chimney, to try and listen to the beating of its wings. Another boy would go up a ladder, outside the chimney. At a given signal, he would beat his chest, and the victim would think it was the bird. While he was looking up the chimney, the one outside would tip a bucket of water down it, covering the victim in soot and water.

Another trick was called *"Pulling the Cat"*. This involved the channel of water from Norton Mere. The cat would be on one side, and the victim on the other. He would have a rope tied round his waist, and told that the others were trying to tie the other end round the cat. He was then told to run. The other boys let go of the cat, and pulled the rope tight, so that the victim ended up in the water.

A third victimisation was called *"Hiding the Noddun"*. A boy was given a rotten egg to hide. Another boy would stay with him, while the others went away, and counted up to an agreed number. The victim would then be persuaded to hide it under his hat. The others would come back. The victim ended up with a squashed hat, and rotten egg all over his head.

Probably some of these games related to different times of year. But the main social event was the Tong Wake. King Henry III, had granted this feast to Tong in 1421, along with a weekly Thursday market. Both events were to be held in the grounds of Tong Manor. The wake was meant to be held on St Bartholomew's Day (24th August), but was transferred to St Matthew's Day (21st September), to ensure the completion of the Harvest. The Wake lasted several days, and involved lots of sports, races and games. These included chasing a pig or a sheep with a greased tail, climbing a greasy pole, and eating treacle buns. The women's races had gowns as prizes. A week before the Wake, everybody would be cooking, and baking pies, puddings, and joints of meat. There were barrels of beer, and much jollity. The Wake ceased around 1870. Along with Christmas parties and the like, such events held the community together. In more recent years, fund raising events have included Flower Festivals, and concerts in the Church. There were other events in the field by the Church, including an *"Old Curiosity Shop"*. Another integrating factors in a community are weddings and funerals. I realised this at one point, when I went for 18 months, without a single occasional office. Funerals are particularly events, when the community reflects on itself, and what individuals have contributed to it. There was a custom at Tong to "Chime the Dead Home". The Church chiming bell began, as soon as the coffin was visible on its way to the Church.

THE SPIRIT OF TONG

The Revd E. J. Gargery (Vicar 1954-54) was very keen on amateur dramatics. He wrote, and produced, a pageant called *"The Spirit of Tong"*. [6] It was performed in the garden of The Priory in the summer of 1950 and attracted many visitors. There was considerable publicity in the Shropshire papers. [7] Gargery brought together many of the stories, that had been handed down at Tong, and perpetuated them in the pageant. The narrative was set in a field near the Church. (See illustration page 146). The characters, in the play, were residents of and visitors to Tong and they encounter personalities from its history. The play is opened, and closed by *"A Stranger"* who at the end, describes himself in these words: the end as:

"I am the Spirit of the ageless Tong-
The upward trend
In Man which seeks that God Who only is
His destined end"

The characters, which are encountered, include Dame Isabella, the Vernons, through to King Charles and Little Nell. Some of the old legends are perpetuated. The character of Dame Elinor Harries speaks of the Tong Cup as a Ciborium:

"which had come from Holbein's day to mine" and she says
"I did bestow a vestment worked with skill
And loving care;
And by Cistercian Sisters, long ago,
Embroidered well."

So the false stories, about the Tong Cup and the pulpit fall as a vestment, are perpetuated. However, Gargery was too much of a Dickens scholar to buy the Little Nell mythology, and simply (like Auden) described her as coming from *"The author's mind"*.

The basic theme of the pageant was based on a Tractarian sense of the continuity of the faith and ministry, within Anglicanism. It was the responsibility of the congregation at Tong to continue this tradition. The characters make a creedal statement about *"the Living Burning Faith"* blazoning forth from an invincible Church. The stranger commends this faith:

> *"For 'tis not Tong alone which speaks to you,*
> *Nor is it I;*
> *It is the call of God to all the world*
> *Since time began,*
> *That man will give his best to Him who gave*
> *The soul of Man."*

The Pageant ended with the singing of Blake's *"Jeruslaem"*. So Gargery made his contribution to preserving the continuity of faith and community. His drama group performed many other plays. There are still those around who took part in them.

NOTES

[1] This material is drawn from Tong Parish Magazines of the period
[2] Auden Vol 1 pp43-47
[3] See Chapter 1
[4] In Shropshire Archives
[5] In his notebook, now in the Shropshire Archives
[6] E. J. Gargery **The Spirit of Tong**
[7] **Wellington Journal & Shrewsbury News** June 10 1950, **Birmingham Post** 5th June 1950 **Market Drayton Advertiser** 9th June 1950.

The photograph on the following page shows the characters in The Spirit of Tong with Margaret Brown as Little Nell; Kenneth Humphries as Sir Richard Vernon; Mrs Wilson as Lady Elinor Harries; Diane Ruscoe as Elizabeth de Pembridge; J. A. Dyer as King Charles II; David Owen and Charlie Owen as monks; Revd A. Wright (of Albrighton) as Sir Arthur Vernon; Revd E. J. Gargery as The Stranger; Kenneth Butler and Dennis Evans as pages.

Cast of the Spirit of Tong

Part Four: Literary Tong

Tong can lay claim to a surprising number of literary connections. Some of these have led to much speculation, and even outright fabrication. They nevertheless provide clues about the imaginative impact Tong has made on generations of residents, and visitors.

Chapter 12

The Shakespeare Connection

The connection with Shakespeare focuses on the Stanley Tomb. Each end has words attributed to Shakespeare:

"Ask who lyes here but do not weep
He is not dead he doth but sleep
This stoney register is for his bones
His fame is more perpetual than these stones
And his own goodness with himself being gone
Shall lyve when earthlie monument is none.

Not monumental stone preserves our Fame
Nor sky aspiring pyramids our name
The memory of Him for whom this stands
Shall out live marble and defacers' hands
When all to tyme's consumption shall be geaven
Standley for whom this stands shall stand in Heaven"

In Chapter 7, we noted how this Tomb has been moved and the connections between the Vernon and Stanley families' history was outlined. But what is the origin of the Shakespearian attribution and can it be justified? The attribution is early. There is a document of 1620 which copies out these words, stating that they are by Shakespeare. [1] Sir William Dugdale, in his survey of Tong in 1663, acknowledged the Shakespearian origin. [2] The Revd R.W. Eyton and Archdeacon Cranage, following him, both have real doubts. Eyton writes about the first verse:

"This was probably an early effort by the poet of genius for Sir Thomas Stanley died in December 1576 when Shakespeare was not yet 13 years old"

On the second verse he writes:

"The opposite end of the Tomb there exist six lines which I cannot but help thinking to have been an imitation of the former and by an inferior poet. Possibly they are in praise of Sir Edward Stanley (son of Sir Thomas) to whose memory the monument is in part devoted for they speak of who lies beneath. Now Sir Thomas Stanley is said to have been buried not at Tong but at Walthamstow."

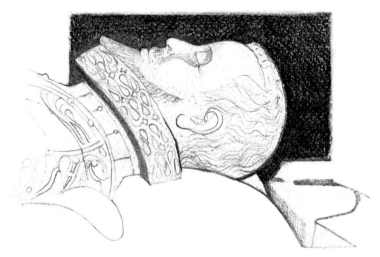

Sir Thomas Stanley's Tomb

This reveals vast confusions. Eyton may not have known that the tomb had been moved. We know that the inscription on Sir Thomas' coffin, which was found in the Sanctuary, confirms that he was buried at Tong. Secondly, the Thomas referred to on the side of the tomb is the son of Edward. Moreover, the inscription on the tomb states that this Thomas died in infancy and is not buried at Walthamstow, but *"in ye parish of Winkle in ye countie of Lancs"*.

In 1929, a Mrs Esdaile wrote a pamphlet entitled **"Shakespeare's verses in Tong Church"**. She asserted the authenticity of Shakespeare's verses. She pointed out that doggerel rhymes, like those on Shakespeare's own memorial in Stratford-on-Avon Church, were written because they were easy for the stone carvers. She mentioned the Shakespeare connection with the Stanleys. **A Midsummer Night's Dream** was written for the wedding of Fernando (Fourth Earl of Derby) in 1588. Fernando had taken over the patronage of Shakespeare's company of players in that year. [3]

Recent research takes us further. In 1985 Prof. E. Honigmann published a book entitled ***"Shakespeare: The Lost Years"***. [4] It contains a whole chapter on the Stanley Tomb. He begins by quoting E. K. Chambers, who dismisses the Shakespearean authorship:

"It is clear that one set of verses cannot be Shakespearean if it relates to Sir Edward Stanley who owned Tong (he died in 1632) and on internal evidence there is no temptation to accept either of them as his." [5]

Chambers is following the errors of Eyton and Cranage. Honigmann is clear that Shakespeare belonged to a Roman Catholic family. When he was 15, his father was made bankrupt. William had to leave school. His schoolmaster put him in touch with his brother, John Cottam, a Jesuit priest, who was working secretly with Catholic families in Lancashire. He was based at Hoghton Hall. Part of this theory relies on the assumption that the reference of a legacy to a servant called Shakeshaft, which appears in Alexander Hoghton's will, refers to William Shakespeare. [6] But there were large numbers of people called Shakeshaft in the Preston area at that time. Ackroyd, in his recent biography of Shakespeare, comments:

"It seems more than a coincidence. What would be more natural than that Cottam should recommend his most brilliant pupil, also a Catholic to be schoolmaster to the Hoghton children." [7]

Hoghton also employed 'players'. There is in existence a copy of Hall's Chronicles, which belonged to Hoghton. It is heavily annotated by a hand which some suspect to be that of William Shakespeare. At this time the Lancashire recusants were being persecuted, this may have led Shakespeare to return to Stratford.

The long connections with the Stanley family make the commission of the epitaph on the tomb more likely, but the dating has confused people. The discovery that the tomb was not erected until 1602 makes the Shakespeare authorship more probable. [8] We should note that there are several other epitaphs by Shakespeare, including his own, with the rhyme of "bones" and "stones". Recently Simon Watney has discovered the tomb of Sir William Gostwick at St Laurence Church, Willington, Bedfordshire. This tomb has the identical first verse as the Tong inscription. This leads him to question the Shakespearian authorship. [9] At the same time there is evidence that the Gostwicks and the Stanleys knew each other, and both had recusant connections. [10] Gostwick may have borrowed the verse from Stanley, or the author may have sold it to both of them. Gostwick died in 1615.

We know that Shakespeare composed at least six other epitaphs, as well as his own. However, the Shakespearean connection with the tomb is not just on the Stanley side: there is also a Vernon connection. The accounts of the Earl of Rutland, for 31st March 1613, records payments to Shakespeare and the actor Richard Burbage for an *"Impressa"* made for the Earl. Burbage was a painter; an Impressa was a symbolic design for a shield. We know that the Earl of Rutland was a friend of the Earl of Southampton, who was a patron of Shakespeare. In the early 1590s Southampton and Rutland were known to *"pass the time in London merely going to plays every day"*. This was Robert Manners 5th Earl of Rutland who died in 1612. The Impressa was made for his brother, the 6th Earl. Dorothy Vernon was the wife of their great uncle and the sister of Thomas Stanley's wife. Moreover, the Earl of Southampton's wife was a Vernon. [11]

The Stanley tomb has also attracted the attention of those who wish to undermine Shakespeare as the author of the plays. One theory ascribes them to William, Earl of Derby, arguing that he wrote the words on this tomb in 1632. The evidence above undermines this and other theories. [12]

In passing we may note two other Shakespeare connections. Both the father of Richard Vernon and the father of Anne Talbot (wife of Henry Vernon) appear in Henry VI Part I in passages relating to the Percy rebellion and the battle of Shrewsbury.

JOHN MILTON

In 1630 John Milton published a poem in Shakespeare's second folio. It has echoes of the verses on the Stanley Tomb. The poem is entitled: ***"An Epitaph on the Admirable Dramatick Poet. W Shakespeare"***

> *"What needs my Shakespeare, for his Honour'd bones,*
> *The labour of an age in piled stones?*
> *Or that his hallow'd reliques should be hid*
> *Under a star-y pointing pyramid?*
> *Dear son of memory, great heir of fame,*
> *What need'st though such weak witness of thy name?*
> *Thou, in our wonder and astonishment*
> *Hast built thyself a live long monument.*
> *For whilst to the shame of slow endeavouring art,*
> *Thy easy numbers flow; and that each heart*
> *Hath, from the leaves of thy unvalued book,*
> *Those delphick lines with deep impressions took;*

Then thou, our fancy of itself bereaving,
Dost make us marble with too much conceiving;
And, so sepulchr'd, in such pomp dost lie,
That Kings, for such a tomb, would wish to die." [13]

Did Milton know about Shakespeare's verse at Tong, or is this simply the sort of architectural/sculptural language current at the time? There were connections. One link was Shropshire. Milton's father's landlord was the Earl of Bridgewater of Ludlow Castle, where **Comus** was performed in 1634. John Milton's father must have known Shakespeare because he became a trustee of the Blackfriar's Theatre in 1608 at the time that Shakespeare's *"King's Men"* were performing there. Milton also knew Alice Spencer, wife of Ferdinand, Earl of Derby. Professor Campbell in an essay on the young Milton also reports on the Stanley Epitaph. [14] At the same time, a recent biographer of Milton refers to *"the Pseudo-Shakespearean verses"* at Tong. We shall never know the truth of this matter. [15]

LADY VENETIA STANLEY, JOHN AUBREY & BEN JONSON

Having referred to Edward Stanley's deceased wife and children the tomb adds: *"ye other three, Petronella, Francis and Venise are still living"*. This last, Venetia, was born at Tong in 1600 and after her mother's death was sent, with her sister Francis, to live at Gayhurst, where her neighbours were the Digby family. As a child, she played with Kenelm Digby. His father was one of the members of the Gunpowder plot and executed in 1606. When Edward Stanley inherited Eynsham Abbey, he moved there with his daughters and Kenelm went abroad. So the Digby connection was severed. She was one of the great beauties of her age, and became the subject of scurrilous comments by the diarist John Aubrey. He says that she stayed at *"Enstone near Oxford"* (he must have meant Eynsham) but *"as private as that place was, it seems her beautie could not lye hid"*. According to Aubrey, all the eligible young men were after her. When she stayed in London, over the door of her lodgings were written the words *"Pray do not come neer, for dame Venetia Stanley Lodgeth Here"*. Aubrey continued:

"She had a most lovely and sweet turn'd face, delicate darke-brown haire. She had a perfect helthy constitution; strong; good skin; well proportioned; much inkling to a Bona Roba (near altogether) her face, a short ovail, darke — browni-brown about which much sweetness, as also in the opening of her eie-lids. The colour of her cheeks was just that of

the damask rose, which is neither too hott nor too pale. She was of a just stature, not very tall." [16]

This leads Aubrey's biographer to comment :

"One would have said that Aubrey was himself in love with Venetia Stanley did one not know that he was only seven at the time of her death in 1633." [17]

Venetia became a well known courtesan, and was for a time the mistress of both the Earl of Dorset and Sir Edmund Wylde of Droitwich. In 1624, she secretly married her childhood friend Sir Kenelm Digby, who she thought had died in a battle at Angers in 1620. Digby was handsome but a very eccentric figure. He wrote cookery books, invented strange medicines, fought battles, and was the model for Ben Jonson's **The Alchemist**. This marriage led Eyton to comment that had Sir Edward retained Tong, Kenelm and Venetia might have inherited. The result might have been even more startling than the antics of the Durants! [18]

After their marriage, she seems to have been a devoted wife, a caring mother, and a supporter of good causes, especially helping poor Catholic families. She died quite young, in 1633, of a cerebral haemorrhage. Aubrey described the event:

"Sir Kenelm had severall Pictures of her by Vandyke etc. He had her hands cast in playster, and her feet and face. See Ben Jonson's 2nd volume, where he hath made her live in poetry, in his drawing of her both Body and mind Sitting, and ready to be drawn

What makes these Tiffany, silkes and lawne,
Embroideries, feathers, fringes, lace.
When ever limbe take like face etc.

She dyed in her bed suddenly. Some suspected that she was poisoned. When her head was opened there was found to be little braine, which her husband imputed to her drinking viper-wine; but spiteful women would say 'twas a viper husband who was jealous of her that she woud steale a limpe." [19]

The poem referred to is **"Eupheme the Picture of her Mind"**. Aubrey gives us the following epitaph to Sir Kenelm, written by a Mr Ferrar:

"Under this stone the matchless Digby lies
Digby the great, the valiant, and wise;
This Age's Wonder, for his Noble Parts;
Skill'd in six Tongues and learned in all the Arts
Born on the day he died th'eleventh of June

On which he bravely fought at Scandaroon
Tis rare that one and self-same day should be
His day of birth, of death, of Victory."

Digby also wrote his own account of his romance with Venetia in a document entitle *"The Courtship of Theogenes and Steliana".*

JOHN EVELYN & LADY MARY WORTLEY MONTAGU

In his diary, John Evelyn (1620-1706) refers to Sir Kenelm Digby as an "arrant mountebank". Evelyn was a cousin of William Pierrepoint. During the Cromwellian period, Evelyn lived in exile. He was a very tolerant Anglican, as well as a Royalist. He is best known for his diaries, which are in sharp contrast to those of Pepys, though often covering the same events. Evelyn also wrote major scientific works, and translated others. In his diaries, he refers to visiting Lady Pierrepoint (the Duke of Kingston's mother) in June 1687 and mentions her death in January 1699. [20]

Another Pierrepoint relative was Lady Mary Wortley Montagu (1690-1762), who was the daughter of Evelyn Pierrepoint. In 1712, she married the M.P., Edward Wortley Montagu. Later, he became British Ambassador in Turkey. She stayed at Tong on several occasions. While abroad, she conducted a detailed correspondence about life in the Ottoman Empire [21] and she adopted Turkish male dress. She left her husband, and fell in love with a young Italian intellectual, Francesco Aigrette. They lived in France, and Italy between 1738 and 1762. She published two volumes of poems in 1712 and was a friend of Addison and Pope. She helped to popularise inoculations for smallpox, by having her own children inoculated. But she was not a very popular figure, and Horace Walpole gives a very unflattering picture of her:

"Her dress, her avarice and her impudence must amaze any one that never heard her name. She wears a foul mob, that does not cover her greasy, black locks, that hang loose, never combed or curled; an old mazarine blue wrapper, that gapes open and discovers a canvass petticoat. Her face is swelled on one side with a pox partly covered with a plaister, and partly with white paint, which for cheapness she has bought so coarse, that you would not use it to wash a chimney." [22]

Griffiths balances this with a quote from Lord Byron:

"And the more than I could dream,
Far less describe, present the very view,
Which charmed the charming Mary Montagu." [23]

NOTES

[1] This is a transcription of the words on the tomb and has a note in a later hand at the top stating *"Inscriptions transcribe in the 1620s"* but the provenance is not at all clear.

[2] See the footnotes on the epitaph in **Complete Sonnets and Poems** ed. by Colin Burrow pp723-4

[3] Esdaile **Shakespeare's Verses in Tong Church**

[4] Honigmann **Shakespeare: The Lost Years**

[5] E. K. Chambers **William Shakespeare - A study of the Facts and Problems**

[6] See also R. Wilson **Secret Shakespeare** and S. Greenblatt **Will in the World**. Too much can be made of the Roman Catholic connection. At this period many people observed religious practices that were most convenient to them Ben Jonson, who was a Catholic for many years and ended up as an Anglican, said he was *"for any religion as being versed in both"*. Shakespeare was godfather to one of his children and probably held similar views.

[7] See Ackroyd **Shakespeare: the Biography** especially Chapters 7 and 15.

[8] See Chapter 7 and Introductory essay to the verse by Stanley Wells in **The Complete Oxford Shakespeare** pp881-2

[9] S. Watney **Sky Aspiring Pyramids**.

[10] I am grateful to Mrs Christine Buckley for pointing this out.

[11] See [7] above p469

[12] One persistent American enquirer wanted the tomb "opened" on the assumption that Edward Stanley was Shakespeare, not knowing he is buried at Eynsham or that the tomb had been moved.

[13] Ed. C. C. Clarke **Milton's Poetical Works**

[14] G. Campbell **"Shakespeare and the Youth of Milton"** in the Milton Quarterly Vol 33 no 4.

[15] G. J. Schiffhorst **John Milton**

[16] Ed. O. Lawson **Aubrey's Brief Lives**

[17] D. Tylden-Wright **John Aubrey a life**

[18] R. W. Eyton **Antiquities of Shropshire**

[19] For the Van Dyke paintings see A. Sumner **Venetia Digby on her Deathbed**

[20] Ed. O. Bray **The Diary of John Evelyn**

[21] Ed. R. Halsband **Selected Letters of Lady Mary Wortley Montague**

[22] C. B. Lucas ed. **Letters of Horace Walpole** p35 for further details of her scandalous life see Julie Peakman **Lascivious Bodies**.

[23] Griffiths p168

Chapter 13
Some Victorian Curiosities

Boscobel House

HARRISON AINSWORTH

Charles Dickens' friend, Harrison Ainsworth (1805-82), was a prolific writer of thirty-nine historical novels. His style was rather like that of Sir Walter Scott, though his dialogue was somewhat stilted. He saw himself writing in the Gothic tradition. In 1827, he met Scott, who had already heard of him, but later described Ainsworth as an *"imitator"*. Ainsworth earned his living as a lawyer, but became a full time writer after the publication of his novel **Rookwood**. It described the adventures of Dick Turpin, and became a best seller. Not taken very seriously by the literary

156

elite, his writings were satirised by Thackeray. If he were alive today, he would be writing scripts for not very good Television plays.

In 1872, he published his novel **Boscobel**. In it, he traced the escape of Charles II, after the battle of Worcester. It is a reasonably accurate, dramatic, account of the events, and refers to Hubbal Grange. [1] In his introduction; he described his sources and said he had spent some time in the area. He had been greatly assisted by *"The Revd George Dodd, Curate of Doddington Salop, the village where Boscobel is situated, who ascertained all the facts connected with the story"*. It was of course Donnington not "Doddington". He visited Chillington, and corresponded with Mrs Jane Llewellyn, the eldest daughter of Richard Penderell, who was the great-great-grandson of John Penderell.

Ainsworth is no longer a significant literary figure, but the effect of his book was to bring the events taking place around Tong and Boscobel into public consciousness, and to attract visitors to the area. [2] However, that cannot compare with the impact made by Charles Dickens in setting the closing Chapters of the *"The Old Curiosity Shop"* at Tong.

THE DICKENS CONNECTION

In the churchyard, near the main door to Tong Church is a grave with a plaque stating *"The reputed grave of Little Nell"*. What lies behind this?

The Old Curiosity Shop was published in 1841. [3] It was previously issued in fortnightly instalments in a paper called *"Master Humphrey's Clock"*. Master Humphrey is the narrator of the early chapters. Readers will be familiar with the story of Little Nell and her grandfather who wander the county seeking solace. The Chapters appeared in fortnightly episodes. They had much the same effect on the public as a TV soap opera, or a radio serial would have today. As the story progressed people wrote to Dickens pleading with him not to let Little Nell die. It became the most famous literary death of the nineteenth century. The following account reveals its impact on the reading public:

"Foster had pressed upon him (Dickens) the artistic necessity of this death and Dickens agreed that it was the only possible ending, but as it began to be foreshadowed in the narrative he was 'inundated with imploring letters recommending poor little Nell to mercy'. He suffered from it so intensely as to feel 'the anguish unspeakable'.

Dickens readers were drowned in a wave of grief no less overwhelming than his own. When Mcready returning home from the theatre, saw the print of the child lying dead by the window with strips of holly on her breast, a dead chill ran through his blood. 'I have never read printed words that gave me so much pain', he noted in his diary, 'I could not weep for some time. Sensations, sufferings have returned to me, that are terrible to awaken…' Daniel O'Connell, the Irish MP, reading the book in a railway carriage, burst into tears, groaned 'He should not have killed her', and despairingly threw the volume out of the train window. Thomas Carlyle, previously inclined to be a bit patronising about Dickens, was utterly overcome. Waiting crowds at a New York Pier shouted to an incoming vessel, 'Is Little Nell dead?'…" [4]

Other critics were less shocked. Ruskin thought it was a blatant piece of marketing. Swinburne thought Little Nell was *"a monster as inhuman as a baby with two heads"*. Aldous Huxley thought it was an example of literary vulgarity. Oscar Wilde said it would need a heart of stone to read of her death without laughing. [5] The first edition of the complete novel sold 60,000 copies with orders for a further 10,000.

In the novel, Little Nell and her grandfather are befriended by the schoolmaster of a village in the Midlands, and they go to live with him. Here Little Nell dies, and her grandfather is subsequently found dead, lying over her grave. Dickens describes the church in some detail. Although it is somewhat romanticised, you can use it to walk around Tong Church. The description bears all the trappings of the picturesque view of Tong promoted by the Durants. When the book was published, they were still in residence at Tong. Here are two extracts:

1. *"If the peace of the simple village had moved the child more strongly of the dark and troubled ways that lay beyond, and through which she had journeyed with much failing feet, what was the deep impression of finding herself alone in that solemn building, where the very light, coming through sunken windows, seemed laden with decay, purified by time of its grosser particles, and sighing through arch and aisle and clustered pillars like the breath of ages gone! Here was a broken pavement, worn so long by pious feet that time, stealing on the pilgrims' steps had trodden out their track and left but crumbling stones. Here were the rotten beams, the sinking arch, the sapped and mouldering wall, the lowly trench of earth, the stately tomb on which no epitaph remained– all– marble, stone, iron, wood, and dust, one common monument of ruin. The best work and the worst, the plainest and the richest, the stateliest and the least imposing– both of heaven's work and man's all found one common level here, and told the common tale.*

Some part of the edifice had been a baronial chapel, and here were effigies of warriors stretched upon their beds of stone with folded hands– cross-legged, those who had fought in the Holy Wars– girded with their swords, and cased in armour as they had lived. Some of these knights had their own weapons, helmets, and coats of mail, hanging upon the walls hard by and dangling from rusty hooks. Broken and dilapidated as they were, they yet retained their ancient form and something of their ancient aspect."

2. *"When the bachelor had given her in connection with almost every tomb and flat grave stone some history of its own, he took her down into the old crypt now a mere dull vault and showed her how it had been lighted up in the times of the monks and how amid lamps depending from the roof, and swinging censers exhaling scented odours, and habits glittering gold and silver, and pictures, and precious stuffs and jewels all flashing and glistening through the low arches, the chaunt of ancient voices had been many a time heard there at midnight in old days, while hooded figures knelt and prayed around, and told their rosary beads, hence he took her above ground again and showed her high up in the old walls small galleries where nuns had been wont to glide along —dimly seen in their dark dresses so far off or to pause like gloomy shadows, listening to the prayers. He showed her too, how the warriors whose figures rested on the tombs, had worn those rotting scraps of armour up above— how this had been a helmet, and that a shield, and that a gauntlet— and how they had wielded the great two-handed swords and beaten men down with yonder iron mace. All that he told the child she treasured in her mind..."*

'A very Aged, Ghostly Place' : The Old Curiosity Shop by Cattermole

Thus is a picture of the church, prior to restoration, and not unlike Petit's description from the same period. [6] The Church may have contained pieces of armour, as did many other Shropshire Churches. We know there was a suit of armour in the Castle. The existence of the College is acknowledged; though the presence of nuns is a literary device. Lowther Clarke considers Dickens description of the country church as *"farcical"*, but he did not know the background. [7] The description fits the Durant imagery, like, for instance, Convent Lodge. All this poses two questions:

Did Dickens set the closing Chapters at Tong? Did Dickens know the Durants? We can go some way in answering these questions.

Archdeacon Lloyd of Salop had met Dickens, who told him he had set the closing Chapters at Tong. A Mr Fletcher wrote:

"I have several times heard him (Archdeacon Lloyd) say – once at the Archidiaconal Congress at Tong– that Charles Dickens told him personally that Tong Church was the church described in 'the Old Curiosity Shop'. But I have forgotten where he met Charles Dickens, but I think it was London." [8]

George Gissing in a critical study of Dickens commented:

"Sufficient evidence is forthcoming to prove that the scene of Little Nell's death was the pleasant village of Tong in the eastern side of Shropshire. The church dating from 1411 was thoroughly restored in 1892. When 'The Old Curiosity Shop' was written its condition was that of picturesque decay, presenting the appearance which is well described in the story. This fine specimen of Gothic Architecture owes to its beautiful monuments the title 'the Westminster Abbey of the Midlands'. There are still extant the original oak choir stalls with the misere seats and carved poppy heads, the old oak roof and sculpture bosses, the wood screens in the aisles of the very rich workmanship and colouring well preserved. The Vernon Chantry, with its remarkable fan traceries once entirely gilt is perhaps the most striking feature of the Church. It is known as the golden Chapel (called the baronial Chapel in the story) owing to its costly ornamentation. Here as well as in the church itself are recumbent effigies… cased in armour as the live memorials to members of the Vernon family." [9]

The Durants knew about the Dickens connection. Griffiths quotes a letter, from Edwin Durant, dated 1884:

"Would it not be well to mention that the sketch of Little Nell in Dickens's work is taken from Tong Church?" [10] But Griffiths does not take this up.

There is another connection. Charles Dickens was born in Portsmouth, in 1812. His grandmother was Elizabeth Ball. She was the daughter of James and Amy Ball, of Claverley in Shropshire. She was baptised there, on

January 10, 1746. Before she married, she was housekeeper at Tong Castle. She married William Dickens in 1781 when she was 36, so she may have been at Tong for some time. After they married, they went into service at Crewe Hall, in Cheshire. So she married just after the first George Durant died. Many biographers say that Dickens and his grandmother enjoyed talking to each other. She died in 1824, when Charles was 12. [11]

Another piece of evidence is an account book from Tong Castle. It covers the period after George Durant (I)'s death, from 1781-4. It is owned by the Ball family, who lived at Tong Norton for many years. They were intermarried with the Salter and Johnson families. One Johnson was tutor to the Durant children. We cannot draw too much from this, but the implication may well be that another member of the Ball family was at the Castle.

It is most likely that Dickens had heard of Tong and the Durants, from his grandmother. But this does not resolve the question of Little Nell. Carleton quotes a Tong tradition that Little Nell was based on Eleanor Lee who died at Tong Almshouses on 9th January 1817 aged 39, and is buried in the Churchyard. He says that Dickens had heard about her from his grandmother. [12] But we do not know when this tradition evolved.

When J. E. Auden arrived as Vicar of Tong, he was anxious to know why people were being shown Little Nell's grave. Why was a fictional character being commemorated? He wrote to his predecessor to ask him. Mr Courtney Clarke replied that, some years previously, Mr Boden, the Parish Clerk, had asked him if there was a grave he could show people as Little Nell's *"because there is money in it."* Clarke would have nothing to do with it. Auden then recounts that, when he was making a plan of the graves, he came across a small grave space with a rough stone marked with the letter "E". Boden asked him if he could show the stone to photographers and visitors, as belonging to Little Nell. He went on:

"I pointed out to him a suitable place to the feeble imagination of those who must have some sentimental picture of a real object in their minds even though it was only a fake." [13]

He denied that he encouraged this tradition. Boden persisted, in spite of the objections. Postcards were sold of Little Nell's House: and also china plates, cups, and teapots were produced. They depicted Little Nell and her grandfather. There was indeed money in it. George Boden could tell a good yarn. One person remembers coming to, Tong when she was aged 8, and being so moved by his heartrending story, she cried all night.

In 1933 George Boden told his yarn to the Wolverhampton Express and Star and the reporter believed it. It is an amazing fabrication. The headline is:

THE VERGER TALKS- *Village LEGEND of the FATE of LITTLE NELL*.

It begins with a description of Little Nell's burial and continues:

Drawing of George Boden
from newspaper photograph

"Even when I stood by the little grave in Tong churchyard I was unconvinced. Every churchyard has its little graves and it is easy to say 'this is Little Nell's'. Then I met Mr Boden.

Mr Boden is 77, though he doesn't look it—and tells you that his mother knew Little Nell and remembers her and her grandfather coming to the village. That is the interesting part of this story. He himself provides the personal link. He then tells you that this is the oral tradition passed on to him by his mother who was the actual witness of these things. And what is the story? He will remind you first of all that Dickens used to visit the old Curiosity Shop in London kept by Nell's grandfather. He was frequently there and became greatly attached to little Nell. Then financial difficulties came upon the old man and the shop was suddenly closed up. Grandfather and granddaughter disappeared in the night. Dickens made up his mind to trace them at all costs, but a long time elapsed before he was able link by link to follow up the chain of their wanderings. As a fact, Little Nell and her grandfather wandered down into the country very much described by Dickens, sometimes living with gypsies, sometimes hitching a lift on a canal barge.

One day Schoolmaster Woods of Tong was on the road between Albrighton and Tong and he came upon the man and the little girl. They got into conversation as they walked together into the village. When they reached the Church, Little Nell asked if they could have a rest there, as they were very tired. They went into the porch and sat down on one of the seats that run along each side. The Schoolmaster asked where they were going to spend the night. Little Nell replied that they did not know.

Next morning the Schoolmaster told the Vicar about his visitors and the Vicar had them down to see him. He resolved to find them a little work. The old man was employed about the Churchyard and the little girl was asked to help in keeping the church clean and they continued to live with the Schoolmaster.

Some months passed and then Little Nell fell ill. Dr Bidwood of Albrighton was called in, but nothing could save her and she died shortly afterwards. She was then 14. She was buried near the porch where she rested on the first evening and the little mound of the grave is still there to this day.

After her death, the grandfather grieved greatly and in the language of the villagers 'went soft'. He told them that Little Nell had gone on and he must leave the village to seek her. For some time they managed to dissuade him, but he would not settle. He said he must go and try and find her. One day he went to the monastery ruins and found a rude stone which he brought and placed on the head of the little grave (where it remains to this day) to mark the spot, if he could not find her. Then he left the village and was never heard of again.

A little time later Charles Dickens came along by the stagecoach and spent the night at what was then an Inn, but is now a private house, immediately opposite the Church. Mr Boden's father had charge of the horses and remembers the visit. Dickens had traced the pair all the way from London but the villagers were only able to tell him that Little Nell had died and was buried and that her grandfather had gone away.

Her little grave is easily found near the porch. It is well kept and upon it the visitor will probably find as I found on my visit, vases of fresh flowers placed there by the children of the village." [14]

This has slight echoes of Dickens' story. There was not a schoolmaster called Woods; Boden's father was a shoemaker, not someone who looked after horses. Though he did have an uncle, born in 1830, who was a blacksmith. More telling is the fact that a careful reading of the novel, reveals that Little Nell was buried inside the church, not outside. There is even a letter, from Dickens, to his illustrator George Cattermole making the point:

"The child has been buried inside the church, and the old man who cannot be made to understand that she is dead, repairs to the grave and sits there all day long, waiting for her arrival to begin another journey. His staff and knapsack, her little bonnet and basket etc lie beside him. 'She'll come tomorrow' he says when it gets dark, and goes sorrowfully

home. I think an hourglass running out would help the nation, perhaps her little things upon his knees or in his hand. I am breaking my heart over this story and cannot bear to finish it." [15]

The Old Curiosity Shop. 'Waiting at the grave' by Cattermole.

<u>Cattermole drawing of the Church Interior in The Old Curiosity Shop</u>

Dickens stayed at Albrighton, not at Tong. Although some say he had not visited before 1840, [16] he was in the area in 1838. On that occasion, he wrote to his wife, describing a journey to Shrewsbury. He said that he had wanted to go via Bridgnorth, but had been compelled to travel *"by way of Wolverhampton"*. Thus, says the commentator, Kitto, *"there is good reason for supposing that Dickens during this tour availed himself of the opportunity of visiting the peaceful and picturesque village of Tong"*. [17]

None of this means that Little Nell is buried at Tong. The continuation of this myth became a running battle between Boden and Auden. So Auden wrote to **The Shrewsbury Chronicle**:

"There is no grave of Little Nell at Tong, for the very simple reason that Little Nell never lived on this earth in the flesh. She was born only in the brain of a very clever

author; and lived only in the pages of his book. 'The Old Curiosity Shop' is fiction from cover to cover, though very attractive fiction as all readers of it must acknowledge". [18]

In a lecture to the Dickens Society in 1932, Auden attributed the whole affair to *"the desire to line Mr Boden's pockets",* and there is substantial local evidence to support this view.

There is one more twist to this story. On my arrival at Tong, I was told that Little Nell's burial was recorded in the Parish Burial Register. By this time the old registers were in the Diocesan Archives. I went to have a look. Bearing in mind that the book was published in 1841, I went through the Register from 1820. At the bottom of a page was a gap clearly left by mistake, which had been filled in. (See illustration page 165). It read:

"Feb 1st Nell Gwyn Tong Hill aged 14 years. J. Isaccson. Officiating Minister."

The entries, on each side, were in faded brown ink. This entry was in thick black ink. The County Archivist looked at it and said, *"That's a forgery- it's Post Office ink".* Here we find the final clue. George Boden was the village postmaster! He did not cover his tracks well. The confusion with Nell Gwyn is laughable. A further check with the registrar of Births and Deaths confirmed that no such burial had been registered. In his lecture in 1932, Auden stated that there was no entry in the register. It looks as if Boden added the entry, after that lecture, to try and rebuff Auden.

But the myth has continued. Christopher Hussey writing in Country Life in 1946 wrote:

"Indeed the grave of one Helen Gwyn who came to Tong with her grandfather and died is pointed out in the churchyard as being that of Little Nell's prototype so that it is not easy to draw the line exactly between fact and fiction." [19]

A television programme about her burial at Tong was made in 1965. However, when the BBC made a television play of the book in 1979, they used another Shropshire Church.

It is worth noting that literary critics are certain that Little Nell was based on Dickens' sister-in-law, Mary Hogarth, who collapsed and died in his arms when she was 17 in 1837. This event was the inspiration for the novel. In a letter, Dickens says he is still grieving for her.

No. 278.	Elizabeth Lee	Tong Salop	Dec. 31.	4 years	J. [...] Rectd
No. 279.	Chamberlain Chevening Ton	Tong Forge	Jan. 17	18 years	S. Fraser, officiating minister
No. 280.	Nell Gwynn	Tong Hill	Feby. 1	8 years	S. Fraser, Curate of Hunt Mumby

The forged entry in Tong Burial Register

Even now, most people only know Tong as the place where Little Nell is buried. The story of Little Nell resonated powerfully with the consciousness of Victorian people. It functioned, in an archetypal way, confronting them, in the person of Little Nell, with the cruelty suffered by children and the poor throughout the century and the resulting burden of guilt on adults. The death, while inevitable, took place within a caring community, and so exemplified the ennoblement of loss. Now, the story of Little Nell has a major place in giving Tong its identity. The story of George Boden's lucrative machinations makes it an even better one.

ELLEN THORNEYCORFT FOWLER

There is also a local author. E. T. Fowler (1860-1929) was born in Wolverhampton, the granddaughter of the first Mayor of Wolverhampton. Her father was also Mayor, later Member of Parliament and the first Methodist to enter the House of Lords as Lord Wolverhampton. They lived in a large house on Wergs Road, Tettenhall. Ellen, and her sister Edith, were privately educated and both became published authors. Ellen began by publishing poetry, but it was her book *"Concerning Isabel Carnaby"* which gave her fame. It was a best seller, with 250,000 copies and 17 editions.

In 1903, she married a schoolmaster, Albert Felkin, who was the son of the manager of Mander's paintworks. They moved to London, and then to Bournemouth. She continued writing novels; all set in the West Midlands, and her last one *"Beauty and Bands"* was published in 1920. She derives her description of places from those around where she lived; but she changed the names. Thus Wolverhampton becomes "Silverhampton", Sedgley becomes "Sedgehill", and Dawley is changed to "Trawley". She knew Tong well, because her uncle, John Hartley, was the tenant of Tong Castle. [20] The Fowler family was well known for their family repartee and wit, and her writings reflect that. The books give a feel of being a mixture of Jane Austen, Oscar Wilde, and Wilkie Collins. Two of the novels refer to Tong (which she called 'Pembruge'). These are: *"A Double Thread"* (1899) and *"The Farringdons"*. The first of these is a complex story involving the Lord Chancellor, twin girls, a stolen diamond, and a clergyman who ends up turning down a Bishopric, to work with the lepers at Robben Island. Reviewing the book The Daily Mail wrote:

"A beautiful story, beautifully told. It scintillates with brilliant dialogue, smart epigram, happy repartee, amusing paradox and wise aphorism. The conversations in the

book are delightfully humorous reading. It will sustain if not greatly enhance the high reputation its accomplished author won last year for her first work 'Concerning Isabel Carnaby'. The novel is little short of amazing for its cleverness and wit." [21]

Another review suggested a comparison with George Eliot. In a later interview Ellen Thorneycroft commented:

"I prefer to deal with real places, though I don't always do so. You are so apt to mislay your rivers or lose a church if you are dealing with a place that exists solely in your imagination".

Tong or 'Pembruge' is not central to either novel. In **'A Double Thread'** there is a failed attempt to get a clergyman the living of Pembruge. But there is a fine description of the village:

"Another day they went by the old coach road to Pembruge, the far famed village of Nell and her grandfather in the Old Curiosity Shop; where the ideal old church is like a miniature cathedral and stands with its ruined college, close by the edge of a lake bespangled with water lilies. At the head of the lake is a fantastically devised castle, like the palace in some quaint old fairy-tale; and all the woods around are a veritable queen's garden of wild flowers, and are in turn paved with marble and gold and amethyst, according as it is the season for snowdrops or daffodils or bluebells. It was too late for spring flowers when Jack and Ethel went to Pembruge; but they wandered through the woods and worshipped in the church, and the stone crusaders there seemed to Jack to be repeating the same message that the warriors at Greystone had already brought- that message of the littleness of temporal and greatness of eternal things." [22]

Her description is accurate. It is interesting that she perpetuates the Little Nell story, and she follows Dickens in talking about crusaders. The book was published while J. E. Auden was the Vicar. He would have known Mrs Hartley.

The Farringdons, published a year later, is set in Sedgehill and is an account of the life of Methodists at that time. Much of the conversation is theological, and may reflect what went on in her parent's home. It contains a description of Pembruge Castle, (given in Chapter 5). So E. T. Fowler's novels show us how Tong was perceived locally. She died, in Bournemouth, in 1929.

P. G. WODEHOUSE

There has been much speculation about the setting of Blandings Castle, the seat of Lord Emsworth, in P. G. Wodehouse's novels. He says that it was in Shropshire and near the market town of Market Blandings. This had hotels and trains to London and was a forty-minute drive from Shrewsbury. Wodehouse spent many years of his childhood at Stableford near Bridgnorth. Members of the Wodehouse Society have spent many years speculating on the matter. The novels give some clues. Blandings Castle was near a river, with a view of the Wrekin in the distance, and had some houses at the gates. Like Fowler, Wodehouse uses alternative names. He mentions 'Badgwick Dingle' (Badger), 'Much Middleton' (Much Wenlock?), 'Rutton' (Ryton), and 'Wrykyn' (Wrekin). They are all in easy reach of Bridgnorth. Many think Market Blandings may be Shifnal. Some have suggested Blandings is Weston Park. In 2003, two geographers at University College, London, thought it was almost certainly Apley Hall. But what about Tong? The Castle would still have been there in Wodehouse's youth, and it is eccentric enough. However, in 1972, Wodehouse stated, *"Blandings was a sort of mixture of places I remembered"*. Tong could well have been one of them, but it has a sufficient story to tell without being mixed up with the Empress of Blandings. [23]

NOTES

[1] W. H. Ainsworth *Boscobel*. Routledge 1872 For Hubbal Grange see Chapter 10. G. A. Henty (1832-1902) also used these events in his novel *Friends Across the Sea*.

[2] Boscobel was attracting visitors even earlier, Defoe in his *A Tour through the Whole Island of Great Britain* (1724-26) mentions travelling there via Watling Street. This almost certainly means that he came through Tong.

[3] There are many editions.

[4] From E. Johnson *Charles Dickens his Tragedy and Triumph*, quoted in W. H. Auden in *The Oxford Book of Literary Anecdotes*.

[5] Introduction by N. Page in *The Old Curiosity Shop* Penguin edition p xi

[6] See Chapter 7

[7] Essay 'Charles Dickens and the Church' in *Eighteenth Century Piety* pp138-141.

[8] Quoted by Auden

[9] G. Gissing *Charles Dickens a Critical Study*

[10] Griffiths page 155.

[11] See Ackroyd in *Dickens* and a paper by W. E. Carlton in a paper for the Dickens Society published in 1961.

[12] See Carlton above.

[13] Auden *Some Erroneous Traditions*

[14] *Wolverhampton Express and Star* 24th August 1933

[15] *Collected Letters of Charles Dickens*

[16] J. H. Clarke's Tong notebook.

[17] See 8 above

[18] *The Shrewsbury Chronicle*

[19] September 30th 1946

[20] See Chapter 5

[21] Quoted in A. Perry *The Fowlers*

[22] *A Double Thread* p199. While it is not clear, it looks as if "Greystone" may be Weston under Lizard.

[23] See the website of the Wodehouse Society.

View of Tong Castle from Ruckley

Epilogue

The dispute between the Revd J. E. Auden and George Boden was a battle about what was true or false. Although Auden left Tong in 1913, he was still writing about it in 1938. An article in **The Birmingham Weekly Post** summarised some of Auden's objections:

"In connection with Tong Church there has been a variously stated to be a crusader's tomb there, which there is not; a peep hole for lepers which is also wrong; precious stones in the NW window of the nave, which consists entirely of glass."

He continues in this vein. The article ends up asking why these legends evolve:

"Reading the manner in which a body of fiction has arisen in the course of living men's memories as related by Mr Auden in this pamphlet one is drawn to reflect on how readily some men's minds run to this sort of invention and how easily legends founded on no facts at all, but the need to impress credulous strangers can arise." [1]

Auden's pamphlet was called *"Some Erroneous Traditions"*. In it he tried to explain how legends arise in a community:

"But how are we to account for the prevalence of baseless legends? Psychologists tell us that their vogue is wing to the working of 'Suggestion' which is one of the most powerful, habitual and subtle factors in all our mental existence. By 'Suggestion' is meant a process of communication resulting in the acceptance of the communicated proposition in the absence of logically adequate grounds for its acceptance. The tendency is to yield without serious question, to the ideas and opinions and persuasions of others is indeed universal. Uncritical people, those whose critical faculties have never been aroused are very open to suggestion and to absorb ideas from it. They are prepared to swallow all that they are told, without thinking, or asking themselves what it really means. This tendency to act or repeat, the assertions of others is called suggestibility and when these assertions are false it is called credulity. Such suggestibility is due to deficiency of knowledge and to the apparently impressive character of the source from which the suggestion is often communicated. This seems to be especially the case when the communicator 'thinks he knows everything because he knows nothing' as the sergeant said of the young corporal. Most of these myths concerning Tong Church may be traced to this latter source." [2]

Auden is drawing on the psychology of his time. There is no doubt that George Boden was the subject of his attack, not only in relation to Little Nell, but also to the multitude of errors in Boden's Guidebook. [3] But Auden simplifies a much more complex matter. He dedicates a section of his **Notes to Folk Lore in Tong** referring to the paranormal with ghosts at Lizard Grange, and Holt Farm; a white hare who turned into a witch, and a child born with wings who flew about the room. [4] Such traditions and myths, along with rituals in the community concerning birth, marriage, death, and the land are an essential part of creating community and always have been. This has been well analysed by Stephen Wilson, showing how slowly such customs died out. They continued longer in rural situations and were perpetuated in one form or another by the Church. [5] Legend and magic fulfil a social function, not least in communities fighting to preserve their identity in changing times.

The enormous impact of the Durants on Tong emerges from a similar background. Aware of Tong's history, caught up in the gothic culture of their age and over anxious to be seen as an aristocratic Shropshire family, they invented a past as old as Roger de Montgomery and scattered buildings with religious connotations around the parish. This led the writers on the Follies of Tong to pose a deep question:

"On first site the follies at Tong present a riddle as to what Durant might have intended with his buildings, decorations and mottoes. Their only reason for existence appears to be their owner's eccentricity, but one wonders whether there may be something deeper to Tong – an iconographic programme, in a rather perverse manner, mocking religion, chivalry and nobility– may be also a celebration of death and decay.

Suddenly it starts to get grim, the obsession with harps, walls, ruins and crosses; the fear and hatred of the children who destroyed mad George's gloating monument on that night of death. Where do jokes end? Where does madness begin?" [6]

Certainly death and decay is part of the story. The Black Death contributed to the building of Tong College. The tombs describe the rise and fall of powerful families. There are stories of war, slavery and corruption. There are accounts of accidents, murders and burials. But we also see a community encountering change and surviving it. Tong seems to fascinate its visitors and its inhabitants. Is it a coincidence that literature also has a central role in the village?

The literary connections are in part due to the power of the owners of Tong Castle but it is more than that. Dickens heard stories from his grandmother, Ainsworth had a romantic view of Charles II, and E. T. Fowler's relatives lived there. But we have to ask why Auden, who left in 1913, spent the rest of his life writing about it. Part of it is the romance, which surrounds the Church and the Castle, but it is also a subtle interaction of the local and the national, the personal and the corporate, the tragic and the frivolous. Here is a sort of human geology built up in various layers, from the Roman settlements to the Norman establishment; from the Vernons, Stanleys and Pierrepoints. There is the Durant layer that is romantic, corrupt, full of falsehood and deceptions. There is the Dickens story and the blowing up of Tong Castle. All this is the stuff of literature.

There are other factors that create a place: geography and landscape are vital elements. Simon Schama [7] examines this matter and points out that most landscapes are the product of human culture. The landscape has many aspects. One is the provision of water. This has been a key aspect of Tong. The river Worfe conditioned the early settlements of Tong. [8] It affected the fertility of the area. Farming, growing, grazing, vineyards and fishponds are related to the provision of water and these activities shaped the landscape. Tong was always very fertile, the sandy south of the south of Tong was used for a crop rotation of turnips, barley, clover and then wheat. The clay soil of the north was a rotation of fallow, wheat and then oats. [9] Similarly a visitor to Tong in the Durant era would have been impressed with the vast amount of water.

Trees and woods also affect the area. The forest at Brewood shaped the area and one tree at Boscobel tells a major story. Wood was essential for building, burning, and so assisted in the development of Tong Forge. Schama points out that both wood and water relate to primitive symbols in the human unconscious. They speak of primitive religion, magic, and to the Christian symbols of death and resurrection. There is of course a "Green man" carved on a misericord at Tong. [10]

Rivers have always been of significance for trade and travel but they were superseded the roads and trains, both of which have shaped Tong over the last 150 years. The Railway line changed the landscape and the M54 motorway even more so. The Roman Watling Street has always provided the northern boundary of the parish.

A third element was rock and stone, without which no community would be what it is. Tong had its own quarry used for much local building and also made its own bricks. Rock also relates to another piece of social cohesion in the strong resistance by the community in 1987 over proposals from Lord Bradford to establish gravel works opposite the Church.

Schama has a section entitled *"Et in Arcadia ego"* dealing with deliberate landscaping. Durant used Capability Brown to make his arcadia even though it was a pale imitation of grander ones. But it reveals the desire of the romantic to beautify the landscape.

Landscape and environment affected the health of the community. A community based on agricultural life is often a healthy one. Fertile land helps to produce healthy food. However some modern farming techniques have not helped. Agricultural chemicals led at one point to the Tong water containing an excessive amount of nitrate. But over the years Tong seems to have been a healthy community. The census figures reveal a long-lived community.

Less easy to define is the way a community is given identity by the way people experience it and talk about it. Tong Village is a distinctive entity, the outlying areas less so. A good view, a fine building, trees and vegetation can lift our hearts or as Tony Hiss puts it:

"particular places around us, if we're wide open to perceive them they can sometimes give us a mental life." [11]

But there must be that willingness to see it. Through it comes the understating that our environment is actually life sustaining. We need a place where we can be. Where we live also conditions what we do and what sort of people we become. This would have been particularly the case in an enclosed feudal environment, but in so far as people can choose where they live, they both mould and are moulded their surroundings. Winifred Gallagher calls this *"psychological ecology"* she quotes the work of Roger Barker looking at people's behaviour:

"The more he watched all sorts of people go about their business in shops, playing fields, offices, churches, and bars, the more certain he became that individuals and their inanimate surroundings together create systems of a higher order that take on a life of their own." [12]

This can lead people to be very keen to maintain things the way they are, and only take to change slowly. This goes some way to explain why people stick to myths and legends. The story has, in some way, become part of their identity.

It is this matter of story, which seems to dominate over all other aspects of what makes up a community. The storytellers sustain it. Every person, every building, has its own story and together they make up the story of the community. The stories are passed on. They are altered and enriched in the telling. Some stories are forgotten. Some are rediscovered. Those who have examined the nature of story, point out that there are only a certain number of basic stories and many of them (like **The Old Curiosity Shop**) involve a journey. Many are essentially the biography of a person or a place. Tong tells its own ongoing autobiography.

In the 1970s in order to raise money for the Church fabric, a pattern was established of offering tours of Tong Church followed by tea in the Village Hall. Originally one or two people conducted the tours, but over the years it has been necessary to increase the number of people to help with this. These people become the *"Village Story Tellers"*. The need to provide them with background information led George and Joyce Frost to transcribe and publish J. E. Auden's **Notes on the History of Tong**, which is the most reliable source of information even though Auden never published them (for years they gathered dust in the Local History Library).

Today, people are very anxious to know their roots and trace their family histories; places are no different. This is not only an historical exercise; it is also a theological one. As John Navone puts it:

"The stories which faith tells are answers to basic questions about the purpose of life and of the world. They situate us within a pattern of meaning interpretative of life and death, nature and history, work and play, individual and community. They orient our lives, appealing to every level of our existence in order to recreate an experience like that, which led to the creation of the story. They express insights into the fundamental images and symbols of our experience, they are concretised expressions of a vision of reality and an affective response to reality." [13]

John Drury got to the heart of the matter when he pointed out that we are story telling and story-listening animals. We have an appetite for the stories God tells us in the lives of others. This appetite for news shows the way we are to live in a mixture of the strange and the familiar. Not only is the Bible full of stories, but also we have our own stories to tell. [14] All this brings cohesion to communities, and families. So we need time to listen, and to tell stories. The community is sustained by the stories and legends it tells about itself. If truth is concerned only with facts, the matter of truth is not central. George Boden was making up a fiction based on fiction; but the story of what he did is itself as good story. His message carries on. A recent website describing Tong says:

"In the churchyard is the grave of Little Nell – True honestly!"

We have already noted that when Elihu Burritt came to Tong in 1860 he summed it up:

176

"Our visit to the little village, which we seem to have stumbled on by accident, was very enjoyable and gave us the satisfaction of an unexpected discovery." [15]

It would not have given satisfaction without all the influences we have noted, and the willingness of the schoolmaster to share the story. Tong needs to keep on telling its story. While some myths may remain, the story is so good it needs little embellishment.

NOTES

[1] ***Birmingham Weekly Post*** October 28th 1935.Stuck in the back of my copy of Griffiths' History of Tong.
[2] J. E. Auden ***Some Erroneous Traditions***
[3] See Appendix G
[4] Auden Notes Vol 1
[5] Stephen Wilson ***The Magical Universe- Everyday Ritual and magic in Pre-Modern Europe*** especially his Introduction.
[6] Headley & Meulenkamp ***Follies*** pp195
[7] S. Schama ***Landscape and Memory***
[8] D. Robinson ***The Wandering Worfe***
[9] See Tithe file for Tong 1837 in National Archive.
[10] See 2 articles by Alcock in bibliography
[11] T. Hiss ***The Experience of Place*** p27
[12] W. Gallagher ***The Power of Place*** Chapter 9
[13] J. Navone ***Towards a Theology of Story*** p31
[14] J. Drury ***The Spirit of Story Telling*** in Theology March 1976 pp78ff.
[15] E. Burritt ***Walks in the Black Country***

Appendix A
Owners & Tenants of Tong Castle

1066 Roger de Montgomery
1094 Hugh de Montgomery
1098 Robert de Belmeis
1102 Richard de Belmeis (1)
1127 Philip de Belmeis (1)
1150 Philip de Belmeis (2)
1159 Ranulph de Belmeis
1167 Alan la Zouche
1190 William de Belmeis
1199 Roger la Zouche
1210 William de Broase
1212 Roger la Zouche
1238 Alan la Zouche
1270 William de Harcourt
1274 Henry de Pembrugge
1280 Fulk de Pembrugge (1)
1296 Fulk de Pembrugge (2)
1326 Robert de Pembrugge
    Fulk de Pembrugge (3)
1364 Fulk de Pembrugge (4)
1409 Richard Vernon
1451 William Vernon
1467 Henry Vernon
1515 George Vernon but Tong occupied by Richard Manners
1568 Thomas Stanley
1576 Edward Stanley who sold Tong to
1603 Thomas Harries
1624 William Pierrepoint
1678 Gervaise, Lord Pierrepoint
1715 Evelyn Pierrepoint (1st Duke of Kingston)
1726 Evelyn Pierrepoint (2nd and last Duke of Kingston)
  Tenants
  1725 T. Crump
  1733 H. Willoughby
  1738 D. Higgs (agent)

1757 F. Carrington Smyth

1764 George Durant (I)

1780 Benjamin Charnock Payne in trust for G Durant (II)

Tenant

E. Plowden

1797 George Durant (II)

1844 George Durant (IV)

1855 Tong Castle sold

1855 George Bridgeman (2nd Earl of Bradford)

1865 Orlando Bridgeman (3rd Earl of Bradford)

Tenant

1858-1909 John Hartley Esq. and subsequently his widow

1909 Contents of Tong Castle sold

1954 Ruins of Castle blown up

Appendix B
The Children of George Durant (II)

(Based on J. H. Clark's notes with revisions from J Bath.)

Married 1) Marrianne Eld of Seighford 7/2/1799 at Tong
Divorced 1825. Marrianne died at Seighford 16/4/1829.

Their children:

1. Marianne b at Windsor 22/11/1799. Bapt at Windsor 15/12/1799.
   died at Seighford 18/3/1800 buried at Tong 26/3/1800.
2. Maria b 1800. d in London 15/4/1833.Buried at Tong 23/ 4/1833.
3. **George (III)** Stanton Eld b at Tong 15/11/1801. Bapt at Tong. He
   married Lucinda Saunders in Paris (d 15/3/1876). 3 children. died at
   Richmond, Surrey 24/9/1831 buried in Tong Churchyard 4/10/1831.
   a) Frances Marianne b 8/10/1827 m William Norcott 4/7/1848
      d1907
   b) **George (IV)** Chares Selwyn b 14/12/1828 married Sarah Greatorix
      in Brussels 24/12/1871 Sold Tong 1855. died 13/7/1872.
   c) Lucinda b1830 m Revd E, Blackett 10/6/1857. d 28/6/1907
4. Arthur Edwin Beaufoy b Tong 24/10/1802. Bapt at Tong 21/11/1802
   pensioned from East India Co Military as Lt 1830. m i) E Harley (6 c) ii)
   C Durant (widow of May Durant) d Gailey 1876
5. Francis Ossian b 20/1/1804 at Tong. Bapt at Tong 11/3/1804
   Ordained 1830. m Cecila Biss 9 children, d 26/7/1869 Buried in Tong
   Churchyard.
6. Edwin Leader b 1805 in Peterborough. Capt in East India Co Miltary
   (Captain) m Elizabeth Buckeridge. 3 children. d 4/11/1844 in India .
7. Eliza Rose Emma Louise born 6/7/1806. Bapt at Tong 10/8/1806.
   Was bitten by a mad dog in Liverpool was paralysed. A fine
   horsewoman who disliked her brothers. d at Tong 24/3/1838 Buried at
   Tong 1/4/1838.
8. Belle Agnes Louisa Durant b 6/9/1807. Bapt at Tong 4/10/1807
   Devoted to her brothers, was engaged to be married to a rich man but
   her father refused to consent. Died at Childwick Hall 6/9/1835 buried
   at Tong.
9. Mark Hanbury b 5/11/1808 Bapt at Tong 4/12/1808. Drowned at
   Tong d a 22 /8/1815. Buried at Tong following a torchlight procession.

10. Bruce Emma b at Tong Castle 9/10/1909 d in Paris 5 /6/1829. buried in Pierre la Chaise Cemetery.
11. & 12. Twins
    i) Bruce Ernest born 1811. Bapt at Tong 9/7/1811. m Mrs Wright of Shackerley Hall. no children. Subject of defamation case in 1839. d 25/3/1846 in London buried in Tong Churchyard. His father's legacy of 2/6d was placed on his coffin.
    ii) Hope Alfred Eugene born 1811 died 14/2/1836 buried at Tong.
13. Anguish Honor Augustus b 17/5/1814. Bapt at Tong 18/11/1814 His name was due to his mother's sufferings giving birth. Lt. in Nottingham Militia. Invented Sweep's patent chimney brushes. m Emma Lord. 6 children. d 1874 in Deal. His son Herbert fell overboard from the ship "Barossa" 10/1/1884 and was drowned, aged 21.
14. May Osmond Alonzo b 1816 Bapt at Tong 2/6/1816. A doctor in Leicester and Ramsgate. m Catherine Galley 22/8/1837. no children. "Found dead in a ditch" at Ramsgate 29/9/1861. Buried at Tong .

George Durant (II)
Married   2) Celeste Lefevre at Tong 25/9/1830. She died in London 1/10/1876.

Their children:

1. Cecil Augustus Caeser born 1831. d 25/3/1832 buried at Tong
2. Celestin b 22/11/1833 m Antoinette Kalona 6 c. d 1872 in India
3. Cecilia b 20/1/1835 d 1910 unmarried
4. Augustine St Alban b 27 Jan at Childwick Hall 1837 m Mary Delpierre 24/9/1868 2 c. d 11/7/1871 in London
5. Alfred b 7/6/1838 d 1853
6. Agnes Julia b 2/4/1840. m E. Tegart 27/1/1870 d 10/10/1903

All but the first of these were baptised at Blackladies R.C. Chapel.

Appendix C

Valuation of the Tong Estate 5th May 1763

Value of estate £ 1115. 7. 2 increased to	£ 1316.	9.	1
Income from Manor of Lapley for Vernon Chantry	£ 0.	15.	6
Stipend of Curate	£ 80.	0.	0
6 widows in Almshouses	£ 12.	0.	0
Cloth for Poor	£ 22.	0.	0
Schoolmaster	£ 4.	0.	0

The Manor Properties	Value	Rent	New Rent
Castle & Garden	£ 16. 2. 2		
3 cottages	£ 51. 2. 5	£ 20. 2. 0	£ 30. 4. 0
Horse Rail Meadows	£ 3. 12. 9	£ 4. 4. 0	£ 4. 4. 0
Pool Meadow	£ 4. 0. 5	£ 5. 0. 0	£ 5. 0. 0
The Cottages Nursery	£ 0. 3. 3	£ 1. 0. 0	£ 1. 0. 0
The Holt Meadow	£ 2. 1. 5	£ 4. 0. 0	£ 4. 0. 0
Old College 3 tenants		£ 3. 0. 0	£ 3. 0. 0
3 Pools		£ 1. 10. 0	£ 1. 10. 0
Desmene Woodlands	£ 102. 0. 3	_ _ _	_ _ _
Park Farm George Steventon	£ 287. 3. 2	£ 140. 0. 0	£ 172. 0. 0
John Jordan			
Tong South Farm	£ 63. 2. 2		
The Mill	£ 77. 3. 0	£ 86. 12. 0	£ 108. 0. 0
Ruckley Grange	£ 124. 15. 0		
Dovecote in Cottage Yard	£ 1. 10. 0		
Mr Blakemore			
Tong North Farm	£ 136. 3. 8	£ 47. 12. 0	£ 60. 0. 0
Sheepwalk on Tong Heath	£ 45. 3. 2	£ 4. 14. 0	£ 6. 0. 0
J. Philips			
The Bell Inn, Farm & Cottage	£ 52. 0. 2	£ 31. 11. 0	£ 40. 0. 0
The Hill Farm	£ 165. 2. 2	£ 68. 14. 0	£ 100. 0. 0
R. Darley			
Hubball Grange Farm	£ 132. 1. 3	£ 49. 10. 0	£ 70. 0. 0
Measehill Farm	£ 152. 1. 3	£ 50. 7. 0	£ 83. 0. 0
J. Carpenter The Woods Farm	£ 202. 1. 11	£ 65. 16. 0	£ 100. 0. 0
J. Dowly The Holt Farm	£ 165. 1. 10	£ 55. 9. 0	£ 80. 0. 0

E. Wright Offoxey Farm	£150. 3. 3	£67.17. 0	£80. 0. 0
W. Tildesley Norton East Farm	£135. 0. 4	£69.14. 0	£78. 0. 0
Middle Farm	£91. 0. 2	£34. 0. 0	£40. 0. 0
Tong Knowl enclosed	£47. 3. 9	£24. 0. 0	£13.13. 0
& sheepwalk			£22. 2. 0
W. Barker Norton Wood Farm	£186. 0. 9	£66. 0. 0	£75. 0. 0
Norton Hall enclosed	£22. 2. 0	£11.11. 0	£6.10. 0
& sheepwalk	£64. 3. 9		£9.10. 0
W. Stubbs			
Lizard Forge, pools and tenants	£6. 0. 2	£11. 0. 0	£16.0. 0
Tong Heath Paddock 2 Cottages	£103. 1. 2	£16. 0. 0	£18. 0. 0
T. Salter Timlet Meadow	£2. 2. 6	£1. 6. 0	£1. 5. 0
R. Fowler Mill &Lands	£8. 2. 6	£24. 0. 0	£24. 0. 0
G. Baddely Cottage & Land	£3. 3. 5	£2. 2. 6	£2.10. 0
Divers cottages		£76.14. 0	£17.12. 0
Widow Tildesley			
Cottage & hide at Tong Norton	£4. 2. 9	£12.12. 10	£3. 0. 0
Chief part of Freeholding		£0.13. 11	£0.13. 11
Great & small Tithes lent to tenants			£108. 6. 9
Some small meadows		£0. 9. 2	£0. 9. 2
Tithes for freeholds	£15. 1. 0	£15. 0. 8	

Appendix D

The Wardens of Tong College

1408	Walter Swann and William Mosse granted land and endowments for the College
1411	William Galley
1413	William Mosse
1418	William Admondeston
1423	Walter Batell
1437	Richard Eyton
1479	Thomas Hynkeley
1490	John Bryken (or Bryton)
1493	Thomas Brown
1498	John Lygh (or Lye)
1508	Thomas Cantrell
1508	Thomas Forster (or Forrester)
1515	Henry Bullock
1526	Thomas Pawson
1535	College Dissolved

Appendix E
Parochial Clergy & Clerks

The Perpetual Curate of Tong became Domestic Chaplain at the Castle. A
new Vicarage was built in 1725. Clergy can be traced as follows:

Incumbents	Assistant Curates
1602-41 George Meeson	William Southall (1640-1)
1641-50 William Southall	
1650-60 Robert Hilton	
1660-66 Joseph Bradley	
1666-78 Richard Warde	
1679-86 William Cotton	
1686-94 John Hulton	
1695-1745 Lewis Peitier	Thomas Hall (1730-45)
1745-48 Thomas Hall	
1748-65 William Brown	
1765-70 Scrope Beardmore	Theophilus Buckeridge (1765-8)
	Rice Williams (1768-70)
1770-91 Theophilus Buckeridge	John Rutter (1770-78)
	H. Addison (1778-9)
	Robert Dean (1779-81)
	Charles Buckeridge (1781-3)
	William Tindall (1783-91)
1791-1807 Charles Buckeridge	George Green (1805-6)
1807-39 John Mucklestone	William Molineaux (1806-31)
	Robert Dean (1812)
	Robert Robinson (1831-39)
	Revd J Dale (1834-38)
	Leonard St George (1838-9)
1839-43 Leonard St George	James Isaacson (1841-43)
	John Wakefield
	T. C. Perry

Tong Vicarage was rented out from 1765- 1843

1843-54 George Harding	John Marshall (1854)
	Henry Bishton (1850-55)
	John Cole (1855-56)

John Harding (1856-70)
George Woodhouse (1856-61)
Benjamin Austin (1861-63)
C. W. Sylvester (1863-64)
Henry Jones (1864-66)
Charles Woodhouse (1867-69)
Francis Walsham (1868)
Edward Barker (1869)
S. Pennington (1869)
John Bagshaw (1870)

1870-76 Richard Lawrence
1877-82 Charles Wilson   Frederick Lyus (1880-81)
1882-90 George Rivett-Carnac
1890-96 John Courtney-Clarke
1896-1913 John Auden
1913-20 William Thomas Milligan
1920-26 Frederick Heaton
1926-35 Arthur Guiness
1935-39 Walter Grove
1939-45 W. W. Holdgate
1945-54 E. J. Gargery
1954-56 J. C. West
1956-61 Brian Skelding
1961-71 Albert Yates
1971-74 John Spencer
1974-76 Henry Follis (also Rector of Blymhill)
1976-77 Graham Johnson (Diocesan Youth Officer)
1978-87 Robert Jeffery (Archdeacon of Salop from 1980)
                              Brian Turnbull (1983-88)
1987-98 George Frost (Archdeacon of Salop)
1998-   John Hall (Archdeacon of Salop)

PARISH CLERKS

Thomas Mayer d 1655
Humphrey Mayer d 1661
Thomas Harrison 1661-1683 (d)
George Harrison 1683-1711 (d)
Michael Ore d 1785
Robert Ore 1785-1826
Robert Tagg d1813 (also Schoolmaster)
Andrew Cousins 1807-1829 (also Schoolmaster)
William Woolley 1813-1829 (son-in-law of Robert Tagg)
Richard McChesney 1839-1846 (also Schoolmaster)
John Wood 1847-51 (also Schoolmaster)
John Longstaffe 1851-71 (also Schoolmaster)
John Boden 1871-93 (d)
George Boden 1893-1939 (d 1943)
Henry Tindall 1939-1976

Appendix F
School Teachers of Tong

1411-1534	Chaplains of Tong College
1725	Thomas Williams (Buried at Tong 1731)
1731	Benjamin Garbett (Buried at Tong 1750)
1793-1805	James Jones (also taught at Tong Norton buried at Tong 1834)
1805	Robert Tagg (Buried at Tong 1813)
1806 (briefly)	William Woolley (Buried at Tong 1856)
1813	Andrew Cousins (Buried at Tong 1829)
1828	Robert MacChesney (Buried at Tong 1846)
1847	John Wood
1851-71	John Longstaff
1872-73	Thomas Henry Duffield
1874-81	James Inglis
1882-1924	Thomas Greener
1924-47	Clara Breese (Buried at Tong)
1947-60	Mrs J. A. Dyer

Appendix G
Guide Books to Tong Church

George Griffiths wrote a guide to Tong Church before the Church restoration around 1890. He then incorporated the material into his *History of Tong and Boscobel* (1894).

Griffiths was Lord Bradford's agent and the book was a sort of celebration of the work done by the new owner of Tong in restoring the Church. Griffiths collected a vast amount of material from various places but the book lack cohesion and often takes the reader off in many byways.

Auden (Vol. 1) refers to a guide by T. P. Marshall (probably the Shifnal printer), which he says is a mixture of Griffiths' book, Shropshire Archaeological, Society Transactions, and an anonymous leaflet called Notes on Tong Church. He lists a large number of errors.

George Boden, the Parish Clerk, produced his own book *History of Tong Castle, Church and College*. This book probably relied on the previous one, but Auden notes the comments of his predecessor on this book as being a conglomeration of pieces from Griffiths, R. G. Lawrence's notebook and he gives four pages of factual errors. It was part of Boden's moneymaking exercises. Auden in his *Guide to Shropshire* gives a good summary of the Church, which was reprinted as a separate leaflet in 1980. J. A. Dyer wrote a short guide in 1960 that sold regularly for 20 years. It was an updated version of Griffiths.

In 1981 I wrote a new Guide to Tong Church correcting earlier errors and written as a tour of the Church. This went through six editions with various amendments. In 2002 the text of this guide was used to produce a fine glossy guidebook *St Bartholomew's Church Tong, Shropshire*, full of pictures and published by R. J. H. Smith of Much Wenlock. This excellent production is now the standard Guide.

Appendix H
Tong Census Figures

Census figures gradually emerged. They became more detailed from 1801. Earlier estimates depended on Bishop Compton's Religious Census of 1675 and the Hearth Taxes of the eighteenth century. Detailed figures are not fully available before 1841. The early data comes from summaries provided in Auden's notes but his summary of total population seems, on checking with the actual figures, to be slightly inaccurate.

1801   The population was 404

1821   The census gives a population of 536. The Village had 100 houses. There were 2 uninhabited houses. There were 261 Males and 275 females. These included 68 families engaged in agriculture and 27 in handicrafts.

1831   This gives a population of 510 with 99 houses (2 uninhabited). There were 253 males and 257 females.61 families were in agriculture and 36 in trade. There were 145 males over 20. 18 were servants and 17 under 20. There were 29 female servants. The trades listed give the impression of a self-contained community. 5 Blacksmiths, 4 Bricklayers, 3 Butchers, 2 Cabinet Makers, 7 Wheelwrights, 1 Clockmaker, 2 Hawkers, 1 Maltster, 1 Miller, 4 Publicans, 4 Shoemakers and 2 Tailors.

1841   This was the first full census where each inhabitant was named. The relationship between people was not given, but can easily be inferred. The records do not give place of birth, but state whether a person was born in Shropshire or not. There is an age discrepancy on some people between 1841 and 1851. The population was 464 (compared with the other figures this look a bit low). There were 227 aged under 20, and 28 aged over 60. There were 14 servants at Tong Castle.

1851   The population was 511, with 222 aged under 20 and 37 aged over 60.

This census gives the relationship to the head of the family. More people are registered as born in Tong than in any subsequent census.

A few farms have Irish labourers. This may be because they arrived as a result of the Irish famine, or because they had been working on the new 1849 railway. The oldest inhabitant was one Joseph Stubbs, aged 96.

1861 The population was 512 with 230 aged under 20 and 49 aged over 60.

The last page of this census is missing. It records the highest average age at 28 years. Not all the children attended school.

1871 The population was 558 with 250 aged under 20, and 53 aged over 60. This records the largest number of houses (122). There were 21 people aged over 70.

1881 The population was 488 with 208 aged under 20; and 37 aged over 60. The number of scholars (schoolchildren) reaches its highest at 110, aged between 3 and 15.

1891 The population was 498, with 201 aged under 20, and 40 aged over 60. So the population has gone back near to the 1841 position, and more houses in Tong than in the surrounding hamlets. It also has the largest number of uninhabited houses. This may relate to changes at the Castle.

1901 The population was 456, with 177 aged under 20; and 36 aged over 60. The population was still dropping. Industrialisation is showing its effect, with a reduced number of labourers. Six of the others are listed as engine drivers, compared with one in 1891. By this time, deep ploughing was done by steam.

1911 Figures are not available.

1921 The population was 421.

1931 The population was 410 in 101 households. This is much the same as 100 years earlier.

1951 The population was 502 in 130 households. The population increased during the war with RAF huts built in the Castle Grounds.

1961 The population was 299. This is in part the effect of the removal of the RAF huts.

1971 The population was 261. This expresses the beginning of radical changes in agriculture.

1981 The population was 250. The agricultural changes were leading to the closure of farms, and farming being done by contract. Also, during this time more people worked outside the village than within it. It became a commuter village. By this time most community activities had ceased.

1991 The population was 249.

2001 The population was 208, with 30 aged under 20; and 58 aged over 60 (including 3 over 90). The average household contained 2.1% people.

There were 38 people with long-term illness, including 21 of working age. There were 38 single people, who have never married and 11 widowed people. The total number of houses was 102, only two more than in 1821. The houses have an average of 7.1% rooms. Only 12 households have no car, and 55 have two or more cars (some with 4). A new shift is seen with 33 self-employed people with 17 of them working from home. Only 18 people were working in agriculture, and roughly the same in manufacturing, with a similar number in real estate and business.

The community is changing again.

Parish or Township of Tong	Name of Street, Place, or Road, and Name or No. of House	Name and Surname of each Person who abode in the house, on the Night of the 30th March, 1851	Relation to Head of Family	Condition	Age of Males	Age of Females	Rank, Profession, or Occupation	Where Born	Whether Blind, or Deaf-and-Dumb
	46 Tong Morton	Edward Jones	Head	Mar	35		Wheelwright	Staffordshire Tettenhall	
		Elizabeth do	Wife	Mar		43		Salop Tong	
		Alexander do	Son	Un	14			do do	
		John do	Son		9			do do	
		Harriet do	Dau			5		do do	
	47 Knowle	Ann Cleeves	Head	W		54	Late school mistress	do Ryton	
		Henry M do	Son	Un	23		Shoemaker	do Tong	
		Lucy do	Dau	Un		14		do do	
		Emily do	Dau			1		do do	
	48 Knowle	Thomas Orr	Head	Mar	48		Gone Mason	do do	
		Mary do	Wife	do		46		do do	
		George do	Son	Un	17		Gentleman's groom	do do	
		John do	Son	Un	15			do do	
		Ann do	Dau			7		do do	
		Joseph Riley	Lodger	Un	21		Agricultural labourer	do do	
	49 Nurcote	Gilbert Cotorage	Head	Mar	48		Farmer of 28 acres employing 6 labs	Staffordshire Albrighton	
		Betsy Mason	Dau	Un		20	Housekeeper	do Yeneton	
		Jos Ralph	do	Un	30		Agricultural labourer	not known	
	House Uninhabited								

Total of Persons ...... 9 | 9

Bibliography

Bibliography of books & papers related to the text of the book.

Published material

P. Ackroyd *Charles Dickens* Minerva 1991

P. Ackroyd *Shakespeare The Biography* Vintage 2005

H. Ainsworth *Boscobel* Routledge no date

F. Anderson *Crucible of War* Faber 2001

M. Ashley *Life in Stuart England* Batsford 1968

K. Aston *An Illustrated Walk Around Pembridge Church* Pembridge PCC no date.

J. E. Auden *Shropshire* Methuen 1912

J. E. Auden *A Short History of the Albrighton Hunt* Arnold 1905

J. E. Auden *Notes on the History of Tong Vol 1* Ed. J. Frost 2003 Arima Press

J. E. Auden *Notes on the History of Tong Vol 2* Ed. J. Frost 2004 Arima Press

J. E. Auden *Tong and Little Nell* Ed. J. Frost 2006

W. H. Auden (ed) *The Oxford Book of Literary Anecdotes.* OUP

E. Ayrton *The Cookery of England* Deutsch 1974

J. Ayto & I. Crofton *Brewer's Britain and Ireland* Weidenfeld & Nicholson 2005

T. J. Barnett & Sons *Tong Castle Catalogue of the Sale of Contents* Whiteman Wolverhampton 1909

J. Bath *Durant of Worcester and Tong* A Family History Australia 1998

G. Beaufoy *Leaves from a Tree* Blackwell Oxford 1930

J. Betjeman & John Piper *Shell Guide of Shropshire* Faber 1951

R. Blunt & M. Wyndham *Thomas, Lord Lyttleton* London

G. H. Boden *The History of Tong Church, College and Castle* (no date or publisher)

B. Botfeld *The Tong Minister's Library* printed privately 1866

O. Bray (ed) *The Diary of John Evelyn* Dent 1973

H. C. Brooke Taylor *The Story of Bakewell Parish Church*

E. Burritt *Walks in the Black Country* The Roundwood Press 1976

C. Burrow (ed) *William Shakespeare: The Complete Sonnets and Poems* OUP 2002

D. Bush *English Literature in the Earlier Seventeenth Century 1600-1669* OUP

J. Byng *The Torrington Diaries* 1781-94 4 Vols. Methuen 1970

Lord Byron *The Poetical Works* F. Warne London no date

D. Carpenter *The Struggle for Mastery* Penguin 2003

H. Carpenter *W. H. Auden: A Biography* Allen & Unwin 1981

194

O. Chadwick *The Victorian Church (2 vols)* A&C Black 1966 & 1970

E. K. Chambers *William Shakespeare: A study of facts and Problems* (2 Vols) OUP 1930

R. W. Chapman (ed) *Boswell & Johnson: A Journey to the Western islands of Scotland* OUP 1978

S. B. Chrimes *Henry VII* Yale 1999

C. C. Clarke (ed) *Milton's Poetical Works* J. Nichol 1861

A. Clifton Taylor *English Parish Churches as works of Art* Batsford 1986

G. H. Cook *Mediaeval Chantries and Chantry Chapels* Phoenix 1947

G. H. Cook *English Mediaeval Parish Churches* Phoenix House 1954

G. H. Cook *English Collegiate Churches* Phoenix House 1959

D. H. S. Cranage *Architectural Account of the Shropshire Churches* Vol II Part ii Wellington 1901

F. H. Crossley *English Church Monuments AD1150-1550* London 1921

D. Cupitt *What is a Story?* SCM 1991

J. G. Davies *Holy Week: A Short History* Lutterworth 1953

H. W. C. Davis ed. *Regista Regnum Anglo-Normannorum* 1066-1154 4 vols Oxford 1913-1969

D. Defoe *A Tour through the Whole Island of Great Britain* Yale 1991

C. Dickens *The Old Curiosity Shop* Penguin Classics 2000 (see also OUP edition)

C. Dickens *The Letters of Charles Dickens* Pilgrim Edition 1980

M. Dobson & S. Wells *The Oxford Companion to Shakespeare* OUP 2001

D. C. Douglas *The Norman Achievement 1050-1100* Eyre & Spottiswoode 1969

E. Duffy *The Voices of Morebath* Yale 2001

C. Dyer *Making a Living in the Middle Ages* Penguin 2003

J. A. Dyer *The Story of Tong Church* 1961

R. W. Eyton *Antiquties of Shropshire* 7 vols London 1854-60

E. T. Fowler *A Double Thread* Hutchinson 1899

E. T. Fowler *The Farringdons* Hutchinson 1900

T. Frost *The Life of Thomas, Lord Lyttleton* Tinsley Bros 1876

W. Gallagher *The Power of Place* Harper 1994

A. Gardner *English Mediaeval Sculpture* Cambridge 1951

A. Gardner *Alabaster Tombs* CUP 1940

E. J. Gargery *The Spirit of Tong* Marshall 1950

W. Gibson *The Church of England 1688-1832* Routledge 2001

G. Gissing *Charles Dickens: a Critical Study* Gresham 1902

P. Glanville *Silver in Tudor and Early Stuart England* Victoria & Albert Museum

R. Gough *History of Myddle* ed. D Hay Penguin 1981

J. Goulianos (ed) *By a Woman: Written Literature from Six centuries by and about Women* Bobbs & Merrill NY (no date)

M. Green *Our links with a Literary Giant* from website on history of Bridgnorth

S. Greenblatt *Will in the World* Jonathan Cape 2004

J de Gruchy *Being Human* SCM Press 2006

G. Griffiths *Guide to Tong Church* 1892

G. Griffiths *Tong Church* 1892

G. Griffiths *History of Tong and Boscobel* Simpkin, Marshall, Hamilton Kent & Co 1894

Guide to Tong Church 2nd revised edition 1985

Guide to Tong Church 6th revised edition 1998

A. Guy (ed) *George Durant's Journal of the Expedition to Martinique and Guadeloupe* October 1758-61

R. Halsband (ed) *Selected Letters of Lady Mary Wortley Montague* Penguin 1986

R. Harbison *Guide to England's Parish Churches* Daily Telegraph 2006

B. L. Harris *Harris's Guide to Churches & Cathedrals* Ebury Press 2006

G. B. Harrison *The Elizabethan Journals* Routledge

G. T. Hartley *Some Notes on the Parish of Lapley-Cum Wheaton Aston* 1912

G. Headley & W. Meulekamp *Follies* J Cape 1986

D. Hey (ed) *The Oxford Companion to Local and Family History* OUP 2000

C. Hibbert *The Personal History of Samuel Johnson* Pimlico 1998

F. Higham *John Evelyn Esquire* SCM Press 1968

C. Hillier *A Journey to the Heart of England* Palladin 1978

T. Hiss *The Experience of Place* Vintage Books 1991

E. Holmyard *Alchemy* Penguin

G. Home *The Parish Church of All Saints Claverley Shropshire* 1947

E. Honigmann *Shakespeare: The Lost Years* Manchester University Press 1985

E. Honigmann *John Weever* Manchester University Press

J. F. Hopewell *Congregation: Stories and Structures* SCM 1987

J. Inge *A Christian Theology of Place* Ashgate 2003

R. Jeffery *St Bartholomew's Church Tong Shropshire* Illustrated Guidebook R. H. Smith 2002

P. Jeffery *The Collegiate Churches of England and Wales* Hale 2004

S. Jenkins *England's Thousand Best Churches* Allan Lane

B. Jonson *Plays & Poems* Routledge 1886

A. Kelly *Mrs Coade's Stone* Self-Publishing Assn 1990

J. Kent *Holding the Fort* Epworth 1978

O. Lawson-Dick (ed) *Aubrey's Brief Lives* Mandarin 1949

J. Lee *Shropshire Parochial Libraries* 1976

W. Leedy *Fan Vaulting; a Study of Form Technology and Meaning* London 1980

B. Lewalski *The Life of John Milton* Blackwells 2003

A. Leggatt *Ben Jonson his Vision and His Art* Methuen 1981

L. Leppard *The Lure of the Local* New Press 1997

D. Lloyd *Arthur, Prince of Wales* St Laurence Ludlow 2002

S. M. Low & D. Lawrence-Zuniga *The Anthropology of Space and Place* Blackwell 2003

W. K. Lowther Clark *Eighteenth Century Piety* SPCK 1945

T. Lynch *Dickens' England: a Travellers Companion* Batsford 1986

C. N. Mander *Varnished Leaves* Owlpen Press 2005

K. H. Mantell *Haddon Hall* English Life Publications 1980

D. McCulloch *Reformation* Penguin 2003

R. March *Catalogue of Sherborne Castle* 1979

Medieval Research Group *Report I: A survey of Watermill Sites in Shropshire* no date

E. Mercer *English Architecture to 1900:the Shropshire Experience* Logaston Press 2003

J. R. H. Moorman *A History of the Church in England* A & C Black 1953

H. Moorwood *Shakespeare and Tong* Arima Press 2007

V. Murray *High Society in the Regency Period 1788-1830* Penguin 1998

J. Navone *Towards a Theology of Story* St Paul Publications 1977

P. B. Nockles *The Oxford Movement in Context: Anglican high Churchmanship 1760-1857* CUP 1994

D. O'Connor *Three Centuries of Mission* Continuum 2000

R. Ollard *The Escape of Charles II after the Battle of Worcester* Constable 1986

C. Osborne *W. H. Auden: The Life of a Poet* O'Mara Books 1995

Oxford Dictionary of National Biography OUP 2004

J. W. Papworth *An Alphabetical Dictionary of Coats of Arms belonging to Families in Great Britain and Ireland forming an Extensive Ordinary of British Armorials* London 1874

J. Peakman *Lascivious Bodies* Atlantic Books 2004

A. Perry *The Fowler Legacy* Wolverhampton 1997

E. Peters *Ellis Peter's Shropshire* Headline 1992

N. Pevsner *Shropshire* Penguin 1958

R. Phillimore & W. Phillimore *The Ecclesiastical Law of the Church of England* 2nd Edition Vol II Sweet & Maxwell 1895

J. H. Plumb *England in the Eighteenth Century 1714-1815*. Pelican 1957

F. Pollock (ed) *Revised Reports 1785-1866* Vol 146 pp1066 ff Sweet and Maxwell 1895

A. Powell *John Aubrey and his Friends* Hogarth 1988

E. Power *Medieval People* Pelican 1951

D. Purkiss *The English Civil War: A Peoples History* Harper 2006.

U. Rayska *Victorian and Edwardian Shropshire from Old Photographs* Batsford 1977

D. H. Robinson *The Wandering Worfe* Waine Research Publications 1980

J. M. Robinson *Treasures of the English Churches* Sinclair Stevenson 1995

I. Roy (ed) *Richard Symond's diary of the marches of the Royal Army* CUP 1997

A. Russell *The Clerical Profession* SPCK 1980

M. Scard *The Building Stones of Shropshire* Shrewsbury 1990

S. Schama *Landscape & Memory* Collins 1995

E. A. Shipman *The Church of St Mary Bottesford* Bottesford PCC no date

E. A. Shipman *Gleanings about the Church of St Mary the Virgin Bottesford* Bottesford PCC 1995

E. Sitwell *English Eccentrics* Dobson

J. Smart *A Description of Tong Castle Shropshire* Wolverhampton 1786

Some Notes on Shottesbrooke Church. No date.

P. Stamper *A Survey of Historic Parks and Gardens of Shropshire* 1980

P. Stamper *Of Naked Venuses and Drunken Bacchanals; the Durants of Tong Castle Shropshire.* In Festschrift for Prof. M Aston.

J. Stevenson & P. Davidson (ed) *The Closet of the Eminently learned Sir Kenelm Digby* Prospect Books 1997

L. Stone *The Family, Sex Marriage in England 1500-1800* London 1977

L. Stone & J. C. F. Stone *An Open Elite England 1540-1880* OUP 2001

D. Stroud *Capability Brown* 1975

M. Swanton (ed) *The Anglo Saxon Chronicle* Dent 1996

R. Talbot & R. Whiteman *Cadfael Country* McDonald 1990

Tong Archaeological Group *Mediaeval Floor Tiles of Tong Church* 1987

Tong Archaeological Group *Mediaeval Floor Tiles* 1977-89

Tong Archaeological Group *Report 1* 1980

Tong Archaeological Group *Report 3* 1982-4

Tong Archaeological Group *Report 4* 1986

R. Towner *Capability Brown and the Eighteenth Century Landscape* Phillimore 1993

B. Trinder *A History of Shropshire* Phillimore 1983

D. Tylden–Wright. *John Aubrey–A Life* Harper Collins 1991

J. W. Tyrer *Historical Survey of Holy Week* OUP 1932

J. Uglow *Hogarth* Faber 1997

P. Ure (ed) *Seventeenth Century Prose 1620-1700* Pelican

Victoria County History of Shropshire Vol II

S. Vayne *Nicholson's Guide to English Churches* English Tourist Board 1984

B. Vickers (ed), F Bacon *The History of the Reign of King Henry VII* CUP 1998

S. Wells & G. Taylor (eds) *William Shakespeare The Complete Works* OUP 1986

J. Westwood & J. Simpson *The Lore of the Land* Penguin Books 2005

A. Wharton *Tong Castle Excavations 1976-79* Tong Archaeological Group 1979

A. Wharton *Tong Castle 1979* Tong Archaeological Group 1979

R. O. Wilson *Secret Shakespeare* Manchester University Press 2004

S. Wilson *The Magical Universe* Hambledon & London 2000

L. Wright *St Leonard's Eynsham* Eynsham PCC 1987

P. Ziegler *The Black Death* Collins 1969

Magazine & Newspaper Articles etc

J. Alcock *Two face masks in the Guildford Museum* Surrey Archaeological Society 1963

J. Alcock *Some Aspects of Celtic Religion in Gloucestershire and the Cotswolds* Bristol and Gloucestershire Archaeological Society Vol 85 1966

M. Allen *The Dickens Family at Portsmouth* The Dickensian No 395 Autumn 1981

J. E. Auden *The Minister's Library in Tong Church, Shropshire* Archaeological Society Transactions 4th Series Vol XII Part I 1929

J. E. Auden *The College of Tong* Transactions of Shropshire Archaeological Society 3rd Series Vol VI 1906

J. E. Auden *Documents relating to Tong College additional notes* S.A.S. 3rd series. Vol VI 1908

J. E. Auden *Ecclesiastical History of Shropshire during the Civil War, Commonwealth and Restoration* S.A.S. 3rd Series Vol VII 1907

J. E. Auden *Three Mytton Letters* S.A.S. 3rd series Vol IX 1909

J. E. Auden *Charles II and Tong* S.A.S. 3rd series Vol VII 1907

J. E. Auden *Some Erroneous Traditions* S.A.S.

J. E. Auden *Tong and Little Nell* Dickens Fellowship 1937

Village Legend of the Fate of Little Nell Wolverhampton Express and Star August 24th 1933

Treasure at Tong Wolverhampton Express and Star 1911

Archdeacon of Salop's Visitation Shrewsbury Chronicle April 14th 1913

Tong Castle demolished as descendant of Gen. Durant looks on Wolverhampton Express & Star 19 July 1954

Tong Priory- a letter from the last occupant Shropshire Magazine Oct 1969

The Spirit of Tong The Wellington Journal & Shrewsbury News 10 June 1950

Ghosts Walk Again at Tong Market Drayton Advertiser 9 June 1950

They Live again in Tong Wolverhampton Express & Star 15th May 1959

R. Smith *The Knell for Little Nell* Birmingham Evening Mail

Bagshaw Directory Shropshire 1851

H. Baker *The Shropshire Follies of George Durant* The Shropshire Magazine no date.

O. J. Benedictow *The Black Death: The Greatest Catastrophe Ever* History Today March 2005

M. J. Bennett *Good Lords and Kingmakers: The Stanleys of Lathom in English Politics* History Today July 1981

G. Campbell *Shakespeare and the Youth of Milton* Milton Quarterly no 33 1999

E. J. Carlos *Shottesbrooke Church, Berkshire* The Gentleman's Magazine 10 1840 Part I pp128-134.

W. J. Carlton *More about the Dickens Ancestry* The Dickensian 1980

The Death and Funeral of George Durant Esq. Shrewsbury Chronicle 6th December 1844

W. A. Carrington *The Will of Sir Henry Vernon* Derbyshire Archaeological Journal vol XVIII 1896

Cole *Gentleman's Magazine*

J. Drury *The Spirit of Storytelling* Theology Vol LXXIX March 1976

Mrs. Esdaile *Shakespeare's Verses in Tong Church* The Times 1929

Gentleman's Magazine 1763

R. E. Heaton *Our Christian Heritage* article in the magazine Evergreen 1982

C. Hussey *Tong, Shropshire* 2 articles County Life 20th & 27th Sept 1946

H. Kirke *Sir Henry Vernon of Haddon Derbyshire* Archaeological and Natural Historical Society, Journal

C. Lines *The Strange Story of Tong Castle* Shropshire Magazine December 1984

C. B. Lucas ed. *Letters of Horace Walpole* Newnes

T. H. McGuffie *A Deputy Paymaster's Fortune* Journal of the Society for Army Historical Research. Vol XXXII No 132 1954

P. Morgan *The Building of Battlefield Church* Shrewsbury Tourism website 2003

H. Nicholson *Saints or Sinners? The Knights Templar in Medieval Europe* History Today December 1994

N. Page *The Old Curiosity Shop*

J. L. Petit *Tong Church Salop* The Archaeological Journal March 1845

Pigots Directory Shropshire 1829

J. S. Roskell *Sir Richard Vernon of Haddon, Speaker in the Parliament of Leicester 1426* Derbyshire Archaeological Society

W. Rubinstein *Who was Shakespeare?* History Today August 2001

Roman Camps in England The Field Archaeology

Salopian *The Blessed Durants* Shropshire Magazine August 1969

Salopian *Shropshire families of Royal Descent* Shropshire Magazine 1979

J. Salter *Tong and the Blessed Durants* Shropshire Magazine

G. J. Schiffhorst *John Milton* Continuum 1990

H. G. Scott *This Little Westminster; the Chantry Chapel of Sir Henry Vernon at Tong, Shropshire* Journal of the British Archaeological Association vol 157 2005

Slater's Commercial Directory Shropshire 1868

A. Sumner *Venetia Digby on her Deathbed* History Today October 1995

H. Thurston SJ *Easter Sepulchre or Altar of Repose?* Article from The Way- no date but probably 1920s

S. Tillyard *Celebrity in 18th Century London* History Today Vol 56 June 2005

Tong Castle demolished as Descendant of Gen Durant looks on Wolverhampton Express and Star 19th July 1954

H. F. J. Vaughan *Ruckley Grange Estate Salop and the families connected therewith* 1879 S.A.S. Vol II pp213-272

S. Watney *Sky aspiring pyramids Shakespeare and Shakespearean epitaphs in early Stuart England* Church Monuments Vol XX 2005

A. Wharton *The Excavation of Tong Castle* Shropshire Magazine 1980

A. Wharton *The Importance of pottery in dating mediaeval buildings* Shropshire Magazine

A. Wharton *There's more to 17th century pipes than Tobacco* Shropshire Magazine 1980

J. D. Winslow *The Old Curiosity Shop: The Meaning of Nell's Fate* The Dickensian Autumn 1981

L. Wright *The Stanley's in Eynsham* The Eynsham Record no 2 1985

Tong Parish Magazine March 1911

Note: *The Gentleman's Magazine*. The quotations in the text of this book are from secondary sources *The Gentleman's Magazine* was the first general magazine in England and was founded in London by Edward Cave in 1731 and lasted until 1907. One of its first writers was Dr Samuel Johnson which may explain the reference in Chapter 3. Many of the articles were written under pseudonyms and one early contributor was the Shropshire writer Richard Gough (author of the History of Myddle). 'Coles' may well be a pseudonym.

Unpublished Papers

Beati Qui Durant: The History of the St George Family Printed in New Zealand
A. Cox *Comments on Revd J E Auden's notes on Tong*
A. Hulbert *The Vernon Chantry, known as The Golden Chapel and related Monuments* January 1981
G. Frost *Talk on Little Nell* given at Tong 2006
R. M. C. Jeffery *The Durants of Tong Castle* A Lecture 1983
R. M. C. Jeffery *The Durants Updated* A Lecture 1987
R. M. C. Jeffery *Prince Arthur, Sir Henry Vernon and Tong* Paper delivered at Prince Arthur Conference at Worcester Cathedral 2002
R. M. C. Jeffery *Uncomfortable Beds* Sermon Preached to the Johnson Society in Lichfield Cathedral 29th September 1998
Particulars of a Fine Freehold Georgian Country Residence Tong House Tong 1968 Duncalfe Hatton and Gardner.
Tong in Literature: A service of readings in Tong Church 29 August 1982
Tong in Literature: Flower Festival Programme 28-30th August 1983
Tong Church Inventory NADFAS Report 1994
A. Wharton *Medieval Floor Tiles at Tong, Shropshire* Interim Report 1983

Archive Material

Durant Family papers (owned privately)
Belvoir Castle Archives
    Transcriptions of Mss.
Essex County Records Office
    T/P195 Church Notes of William Holman of Halstead
Family Records Centre, London
    Tong Census Figures 1841-1901
Lichfield Diocesan Archives
    G. Durant Correspondence with the Diocese of Lichfield 1839
    Licences for Tong Clergy
National Archives at Kew
    E321/46/153 re possession of Tong College
    C1/17/291 Trussell dispute with R Eyton Tong College 1386
    C1/364/22 Dispute between Almsmen of Tong College and former Warden 1500-1515
    MAF 32/640/168 1943 Farm inventory of tong
    IR 18/8312 Tithe Files for Tong 1837
    PROB37/1529 Durant Will Contested 1846-48. 300 pages

NJ90/1312 &J90.1313 Dispute over Tong and Ruckley 1865-7 800 pages

SP46/175/fo 1A 1499 Henry Vernon claim on Richard Ludlow

ED21/14939 School Inspection reports 1871-1914

T164/186/1 Claim by Mr Bird (1938) for annuity granted by King Charles II

IR 30/29/319 Tithe map 1796

E117/10/41 Tong College inventory 1555

PROB20/2052 G Pierrepoint Will 1720

SP 46/181/102 description of Vernon monuments 16th century

C1/887/23 Deeds of lands of the Warden of Tong College 1532-38

C47/7/3/3 Dissolution of Tong College and Bakewell chantry 1547

C143/442/14 Pembrugge foundation Document for College 1400

C205/19/12 Seizure of Whiteladies 1690

C1/1328/8 Dispute between R. Augarde and George Vernon over lease 1553-1555

C1/761/17 Dispute between W Coffyn and G Vernon over manors

E5/18/7 Lease of Lizard grange from Lilleshall Abbey to John Milton

Nottingham University Library

Manvers Papers M3307 nos 1-18

Royal College of Arms

W. Dugdale *Visitation of Shropshire* ms.

Shropshire County Archives

Tong Census Figures 1831,2001

Notebook by Revd R. G. Lawrence (Vicar 1870-6)

Notebook by Mr J. H. Clarke of Tong Norton

Tong School Logbooks

Staffordshire Record Office

SRO.B/A 1/14 Episcopal Register of Geoffrey Blyth

List of Illustrations

204

The colour illustrations on the centre pages of this book show:

1. A portrait of George Durant (1st) painted by Sir Joshua Reynolds in 1761 between his two West Indian expeditions.
2. Belle Isle - a watercolour from George Durant II's notebook.
3. Convent Lodge - a watercolour from George Durant II's notebook.
4. White Oak Lodge - a watercolour from George Durant II's notebook.
5. Knowle Hall - a watercolour from George Durant II's notebook.
6. The Hermitage - a watercolour from George Durant II's notebook.

Index

I

J

K

L

M